American
Mah Jongg
For Everyone

9 九
E 東
W 西

American Mah Jongg For Everyone

THE COMPLETE BEGINNER'S GUIDE

GREGG SWAIN AND TOBY SALK

ILLUSTRATIONS BY WOODY SWAIN

FOREWORD BY GLADYS GRAD

TUTTLE Publishing

Tokyo | Rutland, Vermont | Singapore

Published by Tuttle Publishing, an imprint of Periplus Editions (HK) Ltd.

www.tuttlepublishing.com

LCCN 2020943721

ISBN: 978-0-8048-5247-0

Distributed by
North America, Latin America & Europe
Tuttle Publishing
364 Innovation Drive
North Clarendon, VT 05759-9436 U.S.A.
Tel: (802) 773-8930
Fax: (802) 773-6993
info@tuttlepublishing.com
www.tuttlepublishing.com

Japan
Tuttle Publishing
Yaekari Building, 3rd Floor
5-4-12 Osaki, Shinagawa-ku
Tokyo 141 0032
Tel: (81) 3 5437-0171
Fax: (81) 3 5437-0755
sales@tuttle.co.jp
www.tuttle.co.jp

Asia Pacific
Berkeley Books Pte. Ltd.
3 Kallang Sector #04-01
Singapore 349278
Tel: (65) 6741-2178
Fax: (65) 6741-2179
inquiries@periplus.com.sg
www.tuttlepublishing.com

25 24 23 22
10 9 8 7 6 5 4 3
Printed in China 2205EP

"Books to Span the East and West"

Tuttle Publishing was founded in 1832 in the small New England town of Rutland, Vermont [USA]. Our core values remain as strong today as they were then—to publish best-in-class books which bring people together one page at a time. In 1948, we established a publishing office in Japan—and Tuttle is now a leader in publishing English-language books about the arts, languages and cultures of Asia. The world has become a much smaller place today and Asia's economic and cultural influence has grown. Yet the need for meaningful dialogue and information about this diverse region has never been greater. Over the past seven decades, Tuttle has published thousands of books on subjects ranging from martial arts and paper crafts to language learning and literature—and our talented authors, illustrators, designers and photographers have won many prestigious awards. We welcome you to explore the wealth of information available on Asia at **www.tuttlepublishing.com.**

Stock photo credits

Front & back covers Lars Hallstrom/Shutterstock.com; **Front & back endpapers** bloodstone/istockphoto.com; MaxyM/Shutterstock.com; **Pages 2, 65** JodiJacobson/istockphoto.com; **Pages 14/15 & 96/97** Aleksandr and Lidia/Shutterstock.com; **Page 83** rj lerich/Shutterstock.com; **Page 111** Svineyard/Shutterstock.com

Dedication

This book is dedicated to mahjong teachers everywhere, and to the National Mah Jongg League who've added joy and friendships to our lives since 1937.

Acknowledgments

This book would not have been possible without the support of all our friends and family. We're grateful to Johni Levene and her Facebook Group, Mah Jongg That's It, for helping us form a community. We give special thanks to Amanda Grove Holmén, Karen Walden, Gail Friedlander, Kathy Deane, Mary Paynter, Lolly Swain, Gladys Grad, Debra Castellano, Debra Bachner, and our wonderful book agent Jane Creech.

Contents

Foreword

There's something lovely about the game of Mah Jongg, which challenges its players while allowing them to form wonderful friendships around the table. I've taught many people, and watched them light up when they "get it" and win their first Mah Jongg. It's exciting for them, and for me as a teacher. I've been running National Mah Jongg Madness® Tournaments for years, and seeing players win—and being able to celebrate with them—never gets old. As Gregg Swain says "Everyone should be playing this game!" And now, with this book, they can.

America's history with Mah Jongg came alive in the early part of the 20th century, when the game first came to the States. Almost one hundred years later, Gregg Swain showcased this beautiful art form in *Mah Jongg: The Art of the Game*. Perhaps both the beauty of the tiles, and the mental challenges of the game, have made it one of the fastest growing table games in the country. Gregg and co-author Toby Salk, two wonderful Mah Jongg teachers, have written a book addressing the needs of today's players. They carefully take the reader through explanations of all aspects of the game, almost as if they're standing at the table, working directly with the student. The exercises, activities and quizzes give a deep understanding of all Mah Jongg's facets. The book is a delight to the eyes thanks to the clear and delightful illustrations by Woody Swain. Readers will surely appreciate his complete paper "tile set" based on vintage mahjong pieces. Not only that, but the inclusion of those tiles allows for learning almost as soon as the book is opened. Moreover, a website keeps readers current, with updated answers to questions in the book and information about resources and new rules as they occur.

This book gives more than the basics: there's history, anecdotes and playing strategy. Players will connect with the interesting, thought-provoking, and intriguing nature of the game. Mah Jongg can appeal to the curious and adventurous game player, the potential player who remembers their mother playing, and even the Baby Boomers who would *never* play the game their old Mom played (she was probably in her late 30s at the time). Even young people love it: those Gen X, Y, and Z'ers who cast around for something to stimulate their minds and reconnect them to real people outside the computer screen; college students and high schoolers, and young kids. Players will discover their own passions for the game, and create their own personal histories and communities.

Toby says, "What a treat it is to sit with a group of people and play a mentally stimulating game with beautiful tiles, taking a break from the worries of everyday life. Mah Jongg has brought more into my life than I ever could have imagined."

And now the game can do this for you.

GLADYS GRAD
MAH JONGG MADNESS®
www.mahjongg.org

Preface

The word "mahjong" (MJ) is generic, and refers to the many variations of the game played with mahjong pieces. The universal goal is to put together a winning combination of tiles, thus getting "mahjong." The rituals, scoring, combinations, and even number of tiles, vary the world over. This book will teach you the way The National Mah Jongg League (NMJL) approaches the game of "Mah Jongg." Whenever you see that spelling, we're referring to their type of play. It's the most popular form of the game in the United States, and daily more and more people in the rest of the world are attracted to Mah Jongg.

This book isn't an official guide to the NMJL approach to Mah Jongg and isn't sponsored by or affiliated with the NMJL. It was written because of our love for the NMJL style of play. Those tiny tiles we play with have brought us thousands of hours of joy, and we've formed many long-lasting and close friendships around the Mah Jongg table. We both love teaching the game and introducing others to this pastime. We know what a delightful addition it can be to everyone's life. Mah Jongg allows players to escape their worries and exercise their brains by figuring out which hand to play, developing problem-solving skills. But it's mainly those shared laughs, and the feeling of having a family of friends, that keep us going back to the table, and make us want to share the Mah Jongg joy with everyone we know.

Mah Jongg is good for the mind.

How to Use This Book

Mah Jongg is a wonderful game: it's fun, challenging and exotic. The foreign images on the tiles, and the names of the tiles, can be intimidating to new players, though. Every time we give lessons to new players, we hear the same thing: "I'll never be able to learn all of this." Yet, in a couple of hours, they're playing the game! This book is designed to help you become as comfortable as our in-class students, so that you too can quickly become familiar and confident with the tiles, and the rituals and quirks of Mah Jongg. A caveat: You really need to do the tasks we ask you to. Trust us, they're not daunting.

This book will teach you, the reader, how to play the game. You can master these concepts by yourself, or you can use this book at the same time as you're learning in class. But Mah Jongg is social, and best played with others. Get some friends to learn with you, or if your friends already play, spend time mastering the concepts in this book, and you'll be able to join them in no time!

The National Mah Jongg League (NMJL) has its own approaches to the game, making it very different from other versions. That's what this book is here for: we'll teach you all the ins and outs of the game, and, if you practice and do the exercises, you'll be confident enough to play.

We offer a few new ways a novice player can learn. The back of the book has a couple of wonderful extras. In Appendix E, you'll find a "tile" set you can cut out and use as you're working through the book. The goal of the game is to put together certain combinations of tiles, called "**hands**." Each April the NMJL issues a new "**Card**" (**the Card**) detailing that year's patterns. We've developed our very own timeless Card in Appendix D. It has examples of the types of hands you'll find on the Card each year, allowing you to be familiar with the ways tiles are combined. Working with Our Card you will gain an understanding of how the Card can be used and interpreted.

We begin by introducing you to all the tiles. Soon you'll recognize them without a moment's hesitation, and you'll be ready to move onto the next steps, which we've laid out carefully for you: what to do with the tiles and when. Chapter by chapter you'll add to your comprehension of the game. There are activities to do and questions for you to answer, all leading to a better understanding of Mah Jongg. Soon you'll be able to play and win.

We've laid out the book so that you'll learn by reading, doing activities and quizzing yourself. These icons based on vintage tiles will help:

DO THIS TILE

These activities are quick and easy ways for you to understand the concepts.

ACROBAT TILE

These exercises will take some effort. You'll have to challenge yourself a bit, but by doing so you'll become more familiar with the tiles and the rituals and challenges of the game.

WEB TILE

The Web Tile sets our book apart from other MJ books: we regularly update the information on the book's website: **www.AmericanMahJonggforEveryone.com**. You'll understand the general concepts with this book alone, using our generic Card in the back, but you can visit the website for current information about how tiles in our examples and exercises relate to the NMJL Card. We won't have a copy of the new Card—you have to buy one each year—but you'll see how our tile examples can be shaped into each year's new hands. Our website will also provide you with extra information about the game and its history, and if you read it all, you too can be an expert.

OWL TILE

The Chapter Summary is signaled by the wise owl. Be sure you've absorbed it all before you move onto the next part of the book. Mah Jongg requires cumulative learning; you can't skip ahead. Give yourself time to become comfortable with each chapter before you move onto the next one. It's best if you can spend a few hours each day getting the concepts into your head; if you only give it an hour or two once a week you might forget a lot between sessions.

QUIZ TILE

Most chapters are followed by a quiz accompanied by the talking hawk.

SCHOLAR TILE

Answers to the Quiz are preceded by the scholar.

G&T Time:

Here we—Gregg and Toby—have a chance to share some of our anecdotes, hints and favorite strategies that don't necessarily fit into the logical progression of the text. We want to give our readers as much of an understanding of all facets of the game as we possibly can. We enjoy sharing our love of all things Mah Jongg.

Important words that appear for the first few times are written in **bold**, and defined. Any words in bold will also be found in the Glossary (Appendix C), your go-to place in the book.

Mah Jongg has also given us new friends and hours upon hours of fun, challenges and entertainment. We're sure you'll love it too. What are you waiting for? It's time to Maahj* On!!

Gregg and Toby

*This spelling is the original nickname of this version, featured in the title of Viola Cecil's book *Maahj: the American Version of an Ancient Chinese Game.*

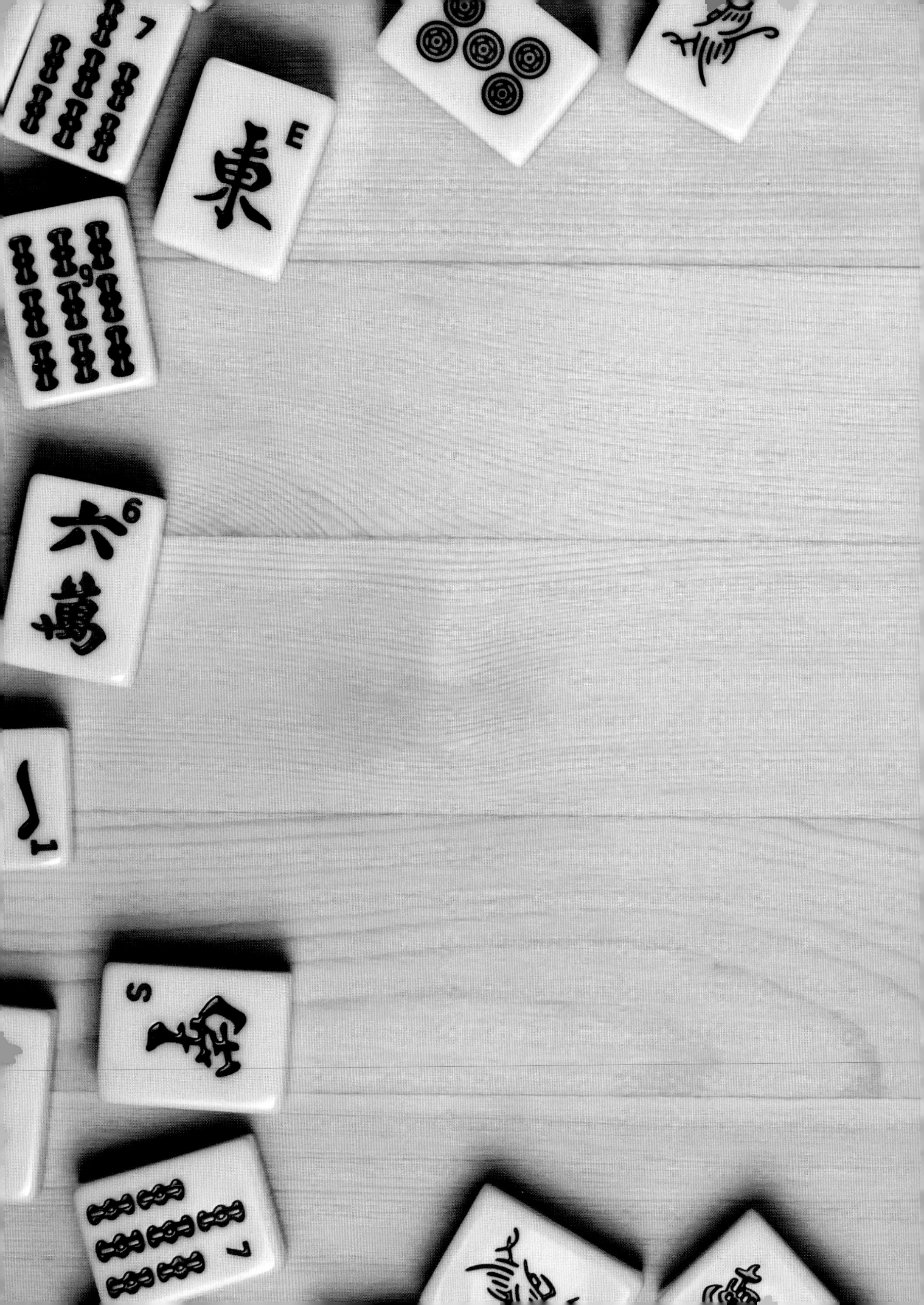

東
E
六萬
6
S

Part 1

History and Fundamentals

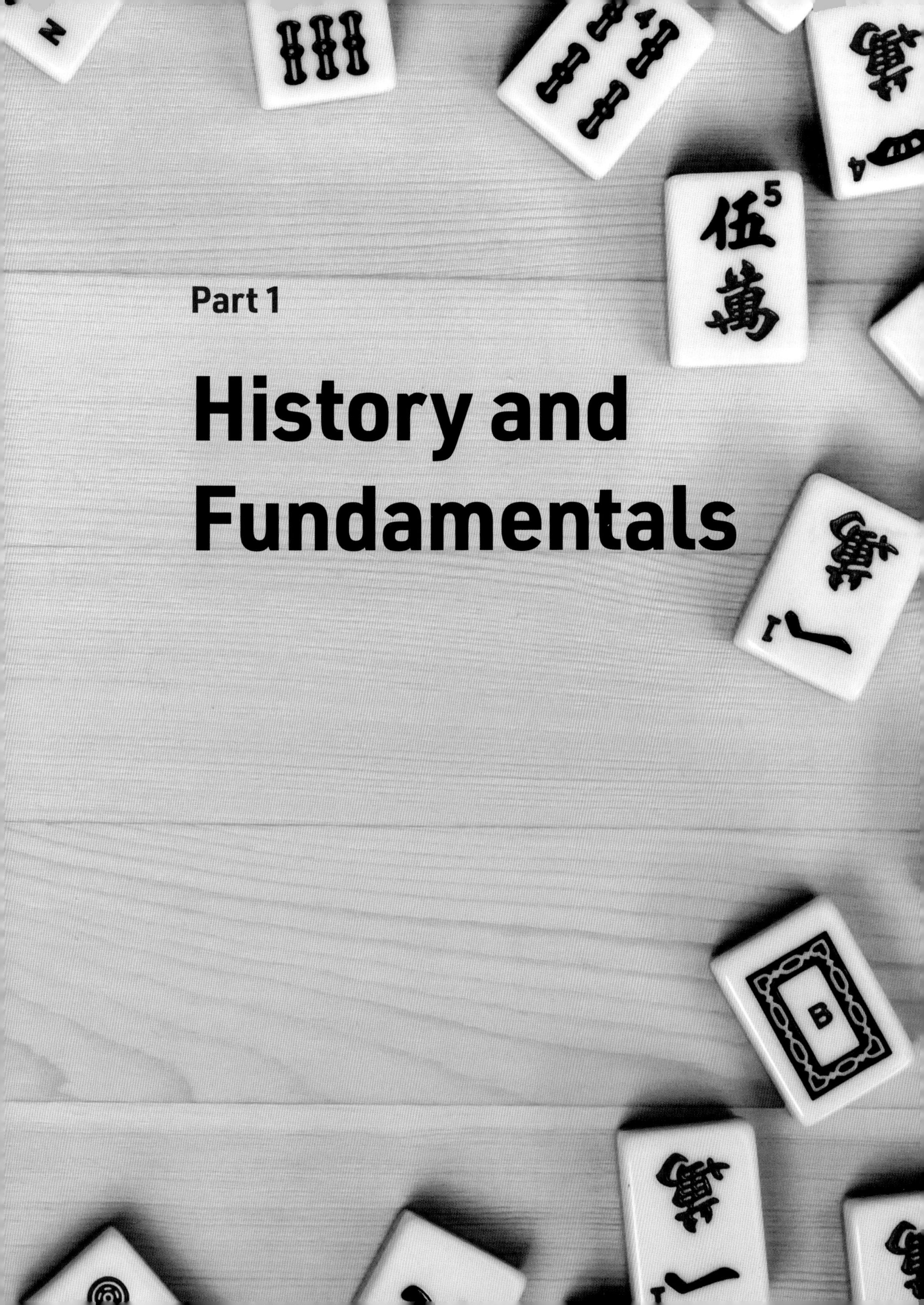

Chapter 1

History of the Game

There are as many stories about the origins of the most popular* game in the world as there are names for **mahjong** (MJ), spellings of the word, and versions of play. "Mahjong" just refers to the tile set itself. In this book, the generic spelling mahjong will be used for <u>all</u> forms of the game. Only when it is written **Mah Jongg** are we referring to the **National Mah Jongg League**'s (**NMJL**) approach.

Mahjong had several precursors—card games starting in the 1300s—none of which exist anymore. They were played by four people working to make patterns with the cards in front of them. The game was social, and mental flexibility was needed. Once it evolved into mahjong in the mid 1800s, all of those elements were still there. Players had to strategize, come up with options, think fast, have backup plans, and anticipate the moves of others. The heart-pumping feeling that the players experience when close to winning, and the adrenalin rush of shouting out "Mahjong," made it addictive from the start.

> Gambling was always part of the game. Fortunes could be won and lost at the table, and many rituals exist to prevent the possibility of cheating. Dice are thrown to determine who the dealer will be, and which tiles will be dealt first.

---

* In 2007, author Kingston Kim estimated there were over 345,000,000 players in Asia alone (www.sloperama.com).

We won't ever know how the tile set, and the idea of making unique combinations, called "**hands**," came about. Because of China's Cultural Revolution, which lasted from 1966 until 1976, there will always be gaps in our knowledge. During that time, historical records and art objects, including mahjong sets, were destroyed. Mahjong became illegal. Virtually the only antique sets we have today are those that were exported from China, or taken out of the country by their owners prior to the Revolution.

In the early days of mahjong, up until the end of World War I, it was mostly unknown outside of China. An American businessman who lived in China, Joseph P. Babcock, is credited with introducing the game to the rest of the world.

Babcock exports Mah-Jongg to the world.

In 1917, workshops in China made mahjong sets, carved by hand, for the Chinese market, with only Chinese numbers and words on the tiles. Babcock thought the game could catch on in the rest of the world, with a few big changes: simplifying the play and scoring. He and others coined the word and spelling of Mah-Jongg, formed the Mah-Jongg Sales Company (MJSC) and in 1920 created their own rules and scoring system. *Babcock's Rules for Mah-Jongg,* or *The Red Book of Rules,* was written. Babcock purchased existing sets from workshops but required the craftsmen to add Western letters and Arabic numbers to the tiles for export. A copy of Babcock's book was included with each set.

Soon the MJSC designed their own set of tiles, with images conjuring up China. Tiles depicted the varied forms of architecture and transportation that existed in that faraway land. Babcock predicted that if there could be an "air of exoticism" about the game, one that would take people away from their cares and worries and give them a bit of an adventure at the same time, Mah-Jongg could be a real success.

> Marketing departments cleverly linked the game to Confucius, the Chinese philosopher. But there was a problem: Confucius had died more than 2,000 years before mahjong came about. Clearly truth was stretched in advertising back in the 1920s! Historical unknowns aside, thousands of sets were exported, and the game began to catch on with players all over the world.

People in the United States and Europe clamored to get sets, and Mah-Jongg replaced Bridge as "the game to play" for a while. Soon other companies took notice: they realized that the MJSC really was only exporting a set of tiles (just like a deck of cards), with copyrighted rules and scoring standards. They thought they too could make and export sets, and they did. Each company was forced to make up a unique name and their own rules and scoring because of Babcock's copyright. The game became so popular that mahjong sets were China's sixth biggest export in the 1920s. Sadly, because everyone was vying for a share of the market (each with their own approaches to the game) mahjong's very popularity led to its downfall: players simply could not agree on one right way to play.

Every company had its own version.

So, almost as soon it burst onto the scene, the mahjong craze was over; but groups all over the world remained loyal to the game they loved. People in different countries

developed their own ways to play, with special hands, tiles, rituals and scoring. Players could win with simple combinations, or more elaborate ones yielding higher scores. The special hands (specific combinations of tiles) kept it complicated enough to be enjoyed by those who wanted more of a challenge.

Given all these differences—country to country, in addition to those instructions included in each manufacturer's sets—it's no surprise that there was a need for a unified American version of the game. Disheartened by people's inability to agree on the way to play, five women got together in New York City in 1937 and formed the National Mah Jongg League (NMJL). Note the spelling of Mah Jongg: two words with two "g"s at the end of the second: it harkens back to Babcock, but without the hyphen. Their goal was to create a version that people all over the USA could play. They combined bits and pieces of other ways to play and came up with their own approach, with the customs and goals we associate with the game today. The **Charleston**, the tile exchange ritual that gave players a chance to shape their hands, became an integral part of the game. **Flowers** were used as wild tiles, filling in for what players were lacking. And most importantly, they printed "the **Card**," the guide to the tile combinations players would strive to put together.

The League wanted people to play the NMJL version so they could have fun together.

The NMJL came up with the idea of generating a new set of hands each year, requiring the purchase of a new Card. Brilliantly, the League dedicated a portion of the Card's cost to charity; Mah Jongg became a guilt-free "charitable" pastime (well, unless the players were neglecting their housework and families!).

Mahjong tiles are a unique form of art, meant to be seen, touched, played with, and heard. While gathered around the table, close bonds develop between the players. People become attached to these small tiles that give them so many hours of joy, explaining why a vintage set isn't sold, but adopted.

The women who formed the NMJL were Jewish, and the game took hold in Jewish communities around the USA. When the League was founded there were fewer than 50 members, but the number grew rapidly. Given its popularity in the Jewish community, it was soon referred to as the "Jewish ladies game." Only in the 2000s did the game start to attract people from all backgrounds.

Over the years the game evolved, and changes were made to the number of tiles needed and how to use them. Rules and scoring were altered. Flowers, which had been wild tiles, became their own category in the 1960s, and **Jokers** were added to take on the wild tile function. By the late 1960s, the number of tiles settled into what we know today.

The NMJL style of play features breaks when players talk and friendships are formed: while tiles are "washed" (mixed) and walls built. After each game the winner receives praise and the others reveal what they'd been trying to achieve. And often losers bemoan (although not for too long) their bad luck. It's those times when laughs are shared, gossip is spread, and relationships are deepened.

And now it's time to start your own personal history with this wonderful game.

G&T Time:

Gregg: I wish I'd played as a teen or young woman. Better late than never!

Toby: I grew up in New York City, in a Jewish family. Our big vacations were going to upstate New York by car to visit my grandparents. This combination was ripe for Mah Jongg, which was affordable and fun. My grandmother, mother and aunts played in the evenings. Decked out in pajamas, we children would say hello, and then disappear. No bridge mix for us! I still remember hiding behind the plastic accordion door on the attic stairs of our tiny house, listening to the wonderful clicking of the tiles. I'd stay up for hours listening to them talk and laugh as they smoked and played the night away. I'm very lucky to be a third-generation player. I feel it in my bones.

Chapter 2

Recognizing the Tiles

Many of us are attracted to the game of mahjong because of the tiles: they're delightful small pieces of art. They're exotic, with Chinese symbols and letters, and many beginning players worry they'll never figure out which tile is which. But we can assure you, if you read this and do the exercises, and really study your tiles, you'll feel comfortable with these diminutive gems by the end of the chapter.

If you have a set of your own, use this book as a guide to become familiar with it. You'll soon learn whether your set is ready for play; if it's not, consult Appendix B. If you don't have one to practice with, turn to Appendix E, where you'll find ours. Cut out the pieces and use them for the exercises until you get a set. Keep our "tiles" stored in a zippered bag.

Some of you may remember how mysterious a deck of cards looked when you first saw one. The clubs and spades looked alike, and the hearts and diamonds were only slightly easier to distinguish. But forget about telling the Jack, Queen and King apart when you're a kid. Mahjong tiles are no different: it'll take time, but recognizing them will become easy. A complete set of tiles for NMJL play has 152 pieces: 36 **Bamboos**, 36 **Characters**, 36 **Dots**, 16 **Winds**, 12 **Dragons**, 8 **Flowers** and 8 **Jokers**. We're now going to look at each kind of tile.

You'll soon identify tiles.

The Three Suits

To begin, there are three **suits**: Bamboos ("**Bams**"), Characters ("**Craks**") and Dots. Each suit has 36 tiles, numbered 1 through 9, with four of each tile. Each numbered tile has a different pattern, although some are easier to see than others. We'll take a look at them one by one. Some of the names of the suits are shortened. Why waste time saying a few syllables when you can get away with one?

Bams

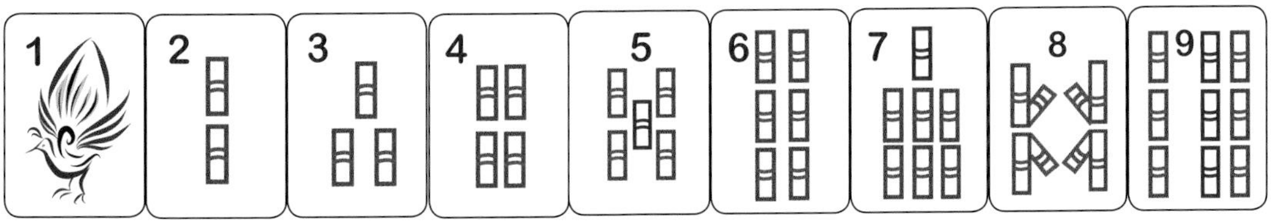

Row of Bams

We'll start with Bamboos, shortened to "Bams," which typically look like sticks or stalks of bamboo, usually green. There are four of each tile, numbered 1–9: four 1 Bams, four 2 Bams, etc.

DO THIS

Place a full row of these tiles in front of you. You'll see each tile has the Bams in different formations. The 8 Bam is always the easiest to make out. (You might get a bit confused by the 6 and 9 Bams, but the 9 Bam has red in the middle.) The 1 Bam might cause you some concern. It's a Bird with a number 1. It's usually a peacock, but it can be a pheasant, eagle, crane, sparrow, swallow, or—be still our hearts—an owl. How are you going to remember that? Just think about a bird flying, eventually landing on bamboo. Or you can always think "Bird Bam." That alliteration always sticks with us. There's an exception, of course. Mah Jongg *always* has exceptions. On occasion you'll see a 1 Bam that looks rather like a pineapple. It's a bamboo sprout and found in vintage sets.

A sampling of the beautiful birds of mahjong.

The best carvers in each workshop would work on the 1 Bam, and often these tiles made people fall in love with, and buy, a set. As a new player, or even an experienced player, whenever you're looking at a set of tiles ask to see the 1 Bam. Mistaking it for another tile is common. Clue: look for a wing or an eye on the tile.

CRAKS

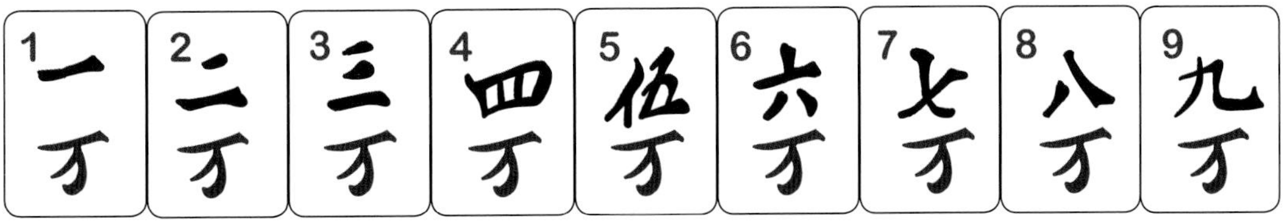

Row of Craks

The next suit is known as the **Craks.** Named after the Chinese word, i.e., the "character" at the bottom of each tile, shortened to Crak. Who wants to say three syllables when one will do?

Craks may look different, such as this one with the ornate Chinese Character. The character can be elaborate or simple, but it's (almost) always red.

Once again, tiles are numbered 1–9, with four of each tile: four 1 Craks, four 2 Craks, etc. Catching on? The Chinese symbols on the tops of the tiles are the Chinese numbers 1–9. Obviously 1–3 are quite easy, but thank goodness Arabic numbers were added so we could recognize them all.

DO THIS

Take out a run of Craks, 1 through 9. Look at them. Beginning players sometimes have a problem distinguishing Craks from Winds (you'll be making their acquaintance soon), but just remember this: if the character is red and at the bottom of the tile, it's a Crak. Take out one each of the numbered Craks, and place them in a line in front of you. Make sure you can recognize these, too.

"It's not a crane, it's a One Bam."

Dots

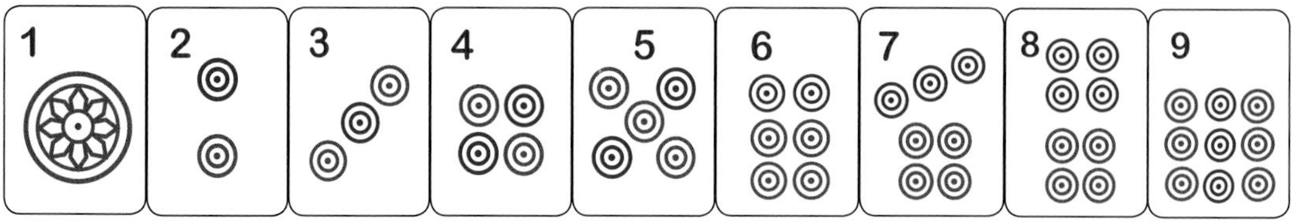

Row of Dots

Dots look like their names. They're numbered 1–9, with four of each tile.

DO THIS

Take out a full run of **Dots**—nine tiles, numbered 1 through 9. Each tile has an Arabic number, and a corresponding number of dots. Place them in a row in front of you. The Dots are in different patterns on each tile, making them easy to recognize once you're familiar with them. Study these tiles for a few minutes until you feel comfortable with the way they look.

Honors

There are tiles we don't think of as being part of one group, but they are: **Honors**. These are **Dragons** and **Winds**. Let's look at the Dragons first.

Dragons

Each Dragon is associated with, or "**married to**," a suit. Given that there are three suits, there are three different Dragons: Green, White, and Red—once again, four of each.

Green Dragon

If you had to guess which suit should get the Green Dragon, we'd bet you'd say Bamboo, because bamboo is green—and you'd be right! In typical mahjong fashion, the Green Dragon has many different looks, but they are all, yes, green.

Different Green Dragons

Although you have a certain type of Green Dragon that comes with this book, you can see from this illustration that the Green Dragon may be figural, but it also might be a character. Sometimes the letter **F** is on the tile, short for Fa: "prosperity."

DO THIS

Find the Green Dragon and put it next to your row of Bams. Hint: Bamboo is naturally green, so it goes with the Green Dragon.

Red Dragon

The Red Dragon can have lots of variations as well, but all of them will be red. Remember how the character at the bottom of the Craks is red? The Red Dragon goes with this suit. (Maybe thinking "firecracker" will help.)

Different Red Dragons

Just like with the Green, the Red Dragon may be figural, or a red character and may have the letter **C** (Chung, for Center, or China) on it.

DO THIS

Find a Red Dragon and put it next to your row of Craks.

White Dragon, aka "Soap"

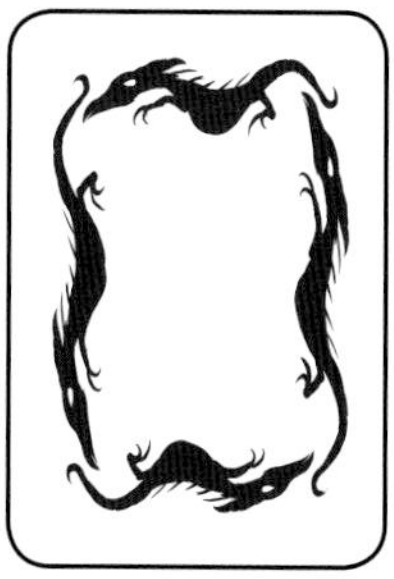

What's left? The White Dragon, which belongs with the Dots. How do you remember the White Dragon goes with Dots? Visualize white polka dots; see if that works for you. Or the shape goes with the shape: the Dot, a shape, goes with the White Dragon, usually somewhat shaped like a rectangle.

Other White Dragons

Of course this Dragon has lots of different looks, too. It can look like a frame, a silver Dragon, or even dragons curled along the edges of the tile. Sometimes there are the letters **P** and **B**, both indicating White: P for Po, and B for Bai. At times the tile is completely blank, looking like a bar of soap, thus its nickname "**Soap**." But no matter what the image is (or isn't), it is always a White Dragon.

DO THIS

Find your White Dragon and put it next to your row of Dots.

The White Dragon is very important in NMJL play: it has two roles. It's associated with the Dot suit. But when it's a **Zero** in a "year hand," it's **neutral.** As a Zero, it goes with

Dots, Bams, or Craks. It is the <u>only</u> Dragon that can be a Zero. (There are always "**hands**" based on the current **year,** and in those years that have "0"s in them—like this whole century—Soaps function as such. In the year 2020, Soaps would be used as Zeros. More later.) How to remember this? White Dragons often look like squared-off Zeros.

DO THIS

Repeat three times: "When the White Dragon is a Zero, it's neutral. It goes with <u>any</u> suit."

EXERCISE

Study these runs of tiles and their associated Dragons. Mix them up and rearrange them, placing the right Dragon where it belongs. Enjoy touching the tiles and listening to them—that's part of the magic of the game.

Winds

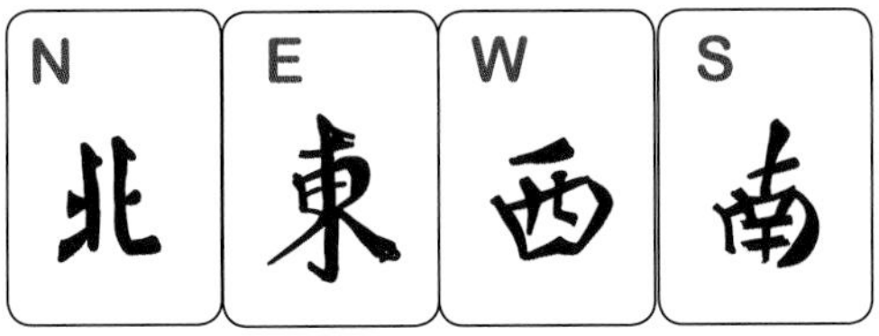

The four Winds

Winds are the second type of Honors. Once again there are four of each: North, East, West, and South, referred to as **N, E, W**, and **S**. Winds are <u>neutral</u>, and <u>not</u> associated with a suit or any other tile. They are affectionately known as "**NEWS**," because you can arrange them in that order. The NMJL likes to have fun spelling out NEWS, so they'll often write the Winds that way.

DO THIS

Get out one of each Wind. You'll notice that there are Western indices on each tile, but there's also a <u>black</u> Chinese character for the type of Wind. The black color helps to make it look different from the red characters on the Craks.

Flowers

Flower tiles

Now we're finished with all the tiles in groups of four: the suits and Honors. Here's the next type: the eight **Flowers** (**F**s). "Flower" is just the catch-all term we give this type of tile. Here's the fun part: the word Flower is a bit of a misnomer: the images can be flowers, but also plants, architecture, types of transportation, Chinese legends, and landscapes, to name a few. Flowers are always neutral, just like the Winds, and not associated with any suit or group. They "play well with others." Because they can go with every type of hand, they're very important. Many of us collectors like them best as they tend to be the prettiest.

All Flowers have numbers on them, and some have partial words. Pay no attention to these markings: a Flower is a Flower is a Flower to NMJL players. In other styles of play, the numbers and words are important, but not in the way we play. The 1 Flower is the same as a 4 Flower or **SPR**, **SUM**, **AUT** or **WIN** Flower (abbreviations for the seasons).

G&T Time:

Gregg: True confession here: I've bought many a set of Mahjong tiles because I have fallen for the Flowers.

Toby: Me too! But now the teacher in me is talking: just remember, a Flower is ANY tile that's a picture, but not a bird or a dragon. If you see a child, an emperor, a maiden, a house, a dog, a cat…it's a Flower.

Some beautiful Flower tiles from vintage sets

One day a young yet very experienced Mah Jongg teacher went to "play with the **Sharks**," players who take no prisoners. Well, our young woman called "Mah Jongg!" and her hand was declared **dead**. (More on that later.) She lost. Not familiar with the tile set, she treated a 1 Bam as a Flower.

DO THIS

Find all your Flowers. If you're using our "tile" set you will only have eight Flowers. If you have a new set, there may be more than eight, so pick out your favorites. (Set the others aside.) Put the Flowers in front of you, and keep looking at them until you feel comfortable. Remember all Flowers are considered identical.

EXERCISE

Take all your Flowers and mix them with your 1 Bam. Now find your Flowers and your 1 Bam. This can be a bit tricky, but you will get it.

Jokers

Different kinds of Jokers

We saved the best for last. The Jokers!! NMJL play uses eight Jokers, but if you have a newer set, you may have more.

DO THIS

Take out your Jokers. Be sure you have eight, and only eight. Jokers may be embossed and original to the set, or tiles may have Joker stickers on them, or there might be red nail polish Js on the tiles! Put away any extras.

If your vintage set is lacking Jokers, or you want to update your Joker stickers, our Appendix B can help.

Jokers are the most "popular" tiles in the set. Why? Because they are the wild tiles of mahjong. They can stand in for any tile. If you need to have three or four of a kind (a **grouping**), and you don't have enough, Jokers can be substitutes. And if you need five or six of a kind, unless it's a group of Flowers, you'll have to use at least one Joker.

But as with all good things, there are important rules about Jokers: Jokers need to be part of a group of three or more identical tiles. You can't use them in a **Pair**, or as a pair, or if you just need one tile (a **Single**) in a grouping. A good way to remember this is "Jokers need a crowd."

DO THIS

Repeat three times "Jokers need a crowd. What's a crowd? Three or more."

EXERCISE

If you have a new set, make sure you have the correct 152 tiles, not too many nor too few of each. If you have extras, put them away—you may need them as replacements someday. You now know which ones you need. If you don't have enough tiles in your set, use the set at the back of the book when you practice, and look at Appendix B for help. Organize all your tiles. Put each suit into its own section, in numerical order, and group your Dragons, Winds, Flowers and Jokers.

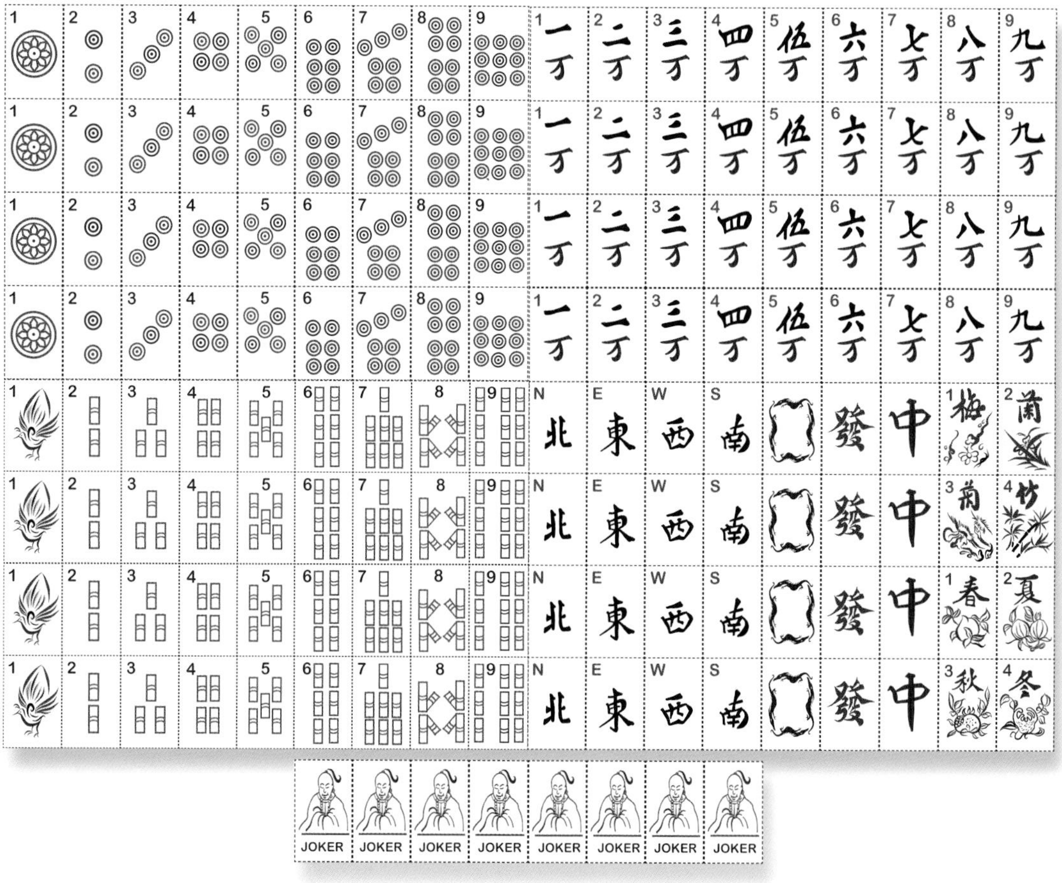

All the tiles from the back of the book arranged by suit and number.

Groupings

The goal of Mahjong is to put the right groupings of tiles together. There are six types of groupings: **Sextet** (six), **Quint** (five), **Kong** (four—think King Kong has four paws), **Pung** (three), **Pair**, and **Single**. Remember: You can use as many Jokers in a hand as you're lucky to get, <u>but</u> you can only use them if you need three or more identical tiles for a group. Your grouping can be all Jokers or a mix of naturals and Jokers.

Now's a good time to get familiar with the abbreviations we'll be using next: **F** is Flower. When <u>next</u> to numbers, **B** is Bam, **C** is Crak, and **D** is Dot. **D** can also represent Dragon if it's alone. You know the Winds. **G** is the Green Dragon and **R** is the Red. **Wh** is Soap when specified as a Dragon, although you won't see that with our Card. **J** is Joker. Don't worry, we'll guide you.

SEXTET

We'll start with a Sextet, which appears from time to time. Let's do Flowers. Find six Flowers and put them in front of you:

FFFFFF

Sextet of Flowers

What would you do if you only had five Fs but you had a Joker (**J**)? Why, use it, of course! You could use up to six Jokers if you had them (although it's not a good strategy).

Now you'll do a Sextet of Norths. You can only do this if you have at least two Jokers, as there are only four Norths:

NNJJNN

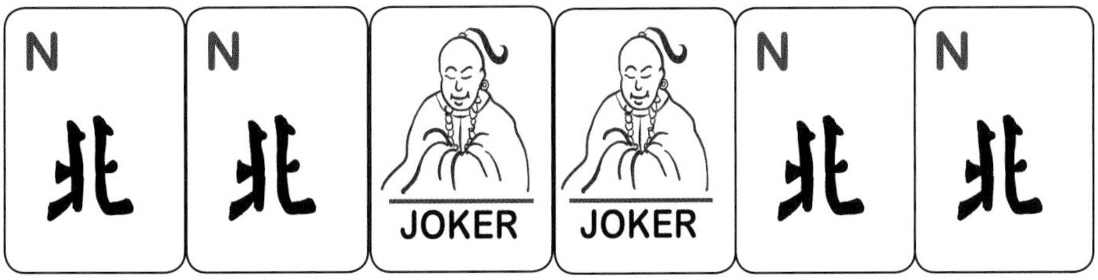

Sextet of Norths

QUINT

The same is true for Quints. Unless you're building it with Flowers, you'll need Jokers.

Flower Quints using all Flowers and with a Joker.

DO THIS

Build a Quint of 8 Bams:

8B 8B J 8B 8B

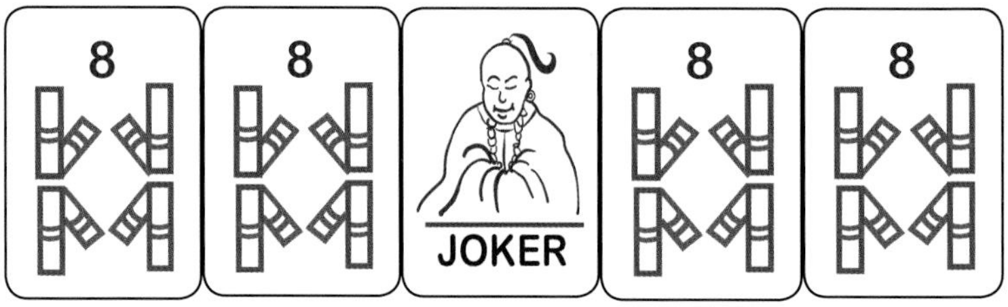

8 Bams Quint

What if you only had three 8s, but you had two Js? That's fine.

DO THIS

Build the Quint using four 8 Bams and then three 8 Bams:

8B 8B 8B J 8B

8B 8B J J 8B

You get the idea.

Kong

On to Kongs, one of the most common groupings on the Card. And because the grouping is four tiles, you can use Jokers.

DO THIS

Take four 9 Dots and put them in front of you:

9D 9D 9D 9D

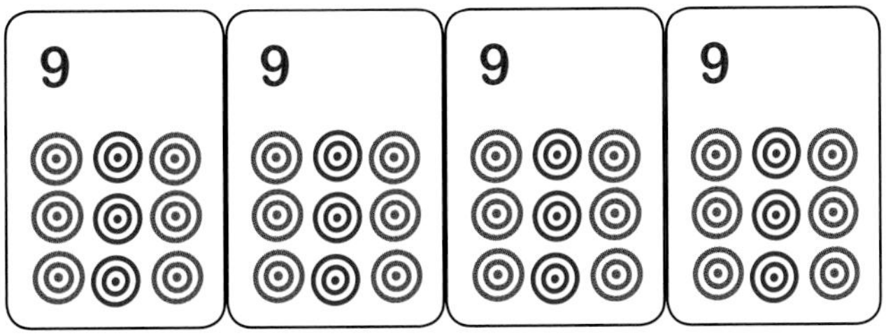

Kong of 9 Dots

Now take away one and put in a Joker:

9D 9D J 9D

Take out another, put in a Joker:

9D J J 9D

Kong with Jokers

You've got this.

PUNG

Now on to Pungs—three of a kind. (We wish there were a mnemonic, but we haven't thought of it!) Jokers can be used here, too.

DO THIS

Take three 8 Bams and put them in front of you. Remove one or two and substitute some Jokers:

8B 8B 8B

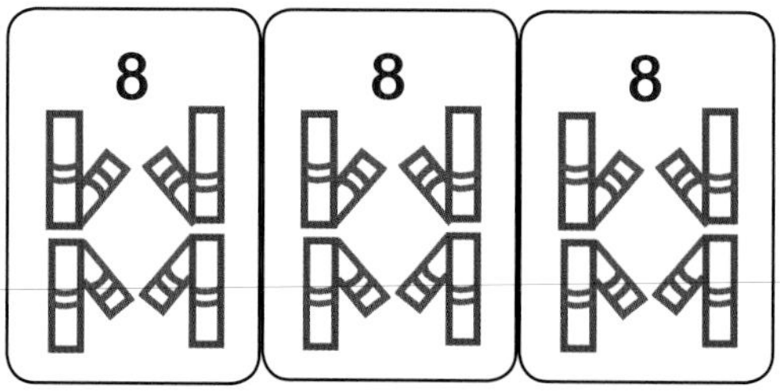

Pung of 8 Bams

8B J J

Pung with Jokers

You can even have this:

J J J

PAIRS

You're now going to Pairs. The big trouble with Pairs is that you must have the actual tiles. Jokers won't do. Take out a pair of Fs, a pair of Dots, a pair of Winds, etc. No Jokers allowed.

No Jokers in a Pair

Singles

You already know what happens with a Single: no substitutions allowed. Jokers can never represent a single tile, and never means never. With special grouping of Singles such as NEWS and the Year, you must have the right tiles. Jokers don't work.

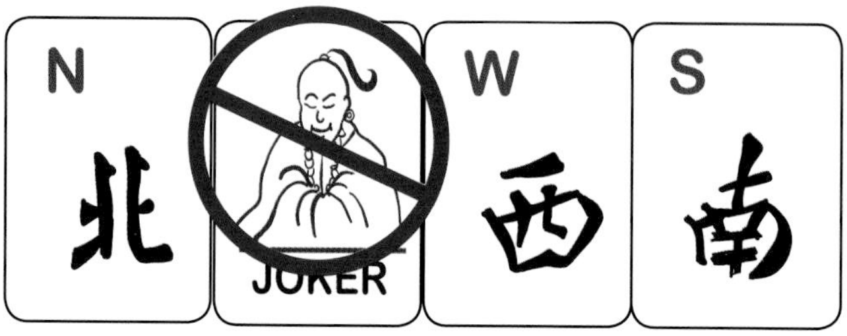

No Jokers anywhere in NEWS

No Jokers anywhere in the year, here 2021

DO THIS

This exercise will get you familiar with how groupings work. To visually sum up what you've learned, here's a chart putting together groupings of 7s of the same suit. Take out four 7 Craks, and six Jokers. You'll understand how this works once you go through this exercise. Make each of these.

Sextet	Quint	Kong	Pung	Pair	Single
7777JJ	7777J	7777	777	77	7
777JJJ	777JJ	777J	77J		
77JJJJ	77JJJ	77JJ	7JJ		
7JJJJJ	7JJJJ	7JJJ	JJJ		
JJJJJJ	JJJJJ	JJJJ			

For the Pair and the Single you may not use a Joker. You must have the required tiles.

Summary

- 152 tiles are needed for play.
- There are three suits: Bams, Craks, and Dots, numbered 1–9, with four of each tile. You'll also find three types of Dragons: Green, Red, and White, four of each. They can be figural or Chinese words. Each color Dragon goes with a specific suit: Green with Bams (bamboo is green), Red with Craks (firecrackers), White with Dots (white polka dots). White's nickname is "Soap." The Soap does double duty: it's a Dragon, or a Zero in "Years Hands."
- The Winds are North, East, West, and South, four of each. They are abbreviated N E W and S on the tiles and the Card, and they are affectionately known as "NEWS."
- Eight Flowers are needed for play. The tiles usually have numbers on them, and sometimes partial words, but pay no attention: a Flower (F) is a Flower.
- Happily, there are eight Jokers. They can substitute for any tiles but never can be used in a pair, as a pair, as a single tile, or in special groupings such as the year (2021, for example) or NEWS.
- Play involves putting together certain groupings of Sextets (six of a kind), Quints (five of a kind), Kongs (four of a kind) along with Pairs and Singles and Pungs (three of a kind). Jokers can be part of groupings, but Pairs and Singles must be made from the actual tiles: no Jokers allowed.

Exercise

Make a Kong of **Ds** using Red Dragons and two Js: **DDJJ**

Make a Pung of Wests using one J: **WWJ**

Make a Sextet of 6s using three Bams and three Js: **6B 6B 6B JJJ**

Make a Quint of Flowers without using any Js: **FFFFF**

Make a Sextet of Flowers using two Js: **FFFFJJ**

Make a Pair of Green Dragons (G): **GG**

Make a Kong of Red Dragons using one J: **DDDJ**

Put out a Pung of 4 Craks and a Pung of matching Ds. Use two Js anywhere:
4C 4CJ DDJ or **4CJJ DDD** or **4C 4C 4C DJJ**

Using 2 Jokers, make a Kong of 9 Dots and a Pair of matching Dragons (there is only one right way to do this): **9D 9DJJ** and **DD** (two Whs.)

Quiz

1 How many tiles are used for NMJL play?

2 How many suits are there?

3 How many tiles in each suit?

4 The numbers on the suit tiles go from what number to what number?

5 What do N, E, W, and S stand for? How many of each are there?

6 What does F stand for on the card?

7 How many Flowers are there?

8 Do the shortened words or numbers on the Flowers tile make a difference?

9 What tile is nicknamed "Soap"?

10 Can you ever use one or two Jokers in a Pair? Can you use one Joker as a Single?

11 What does the 1 Bam look like?

12 What suit does the Red Dragon go with? How about the Green? And the White?

13 Which tiles are always neutral?

14 Which tiles are sometimes neutral?

Answers

1 152.

2 Three.

3 36 tiles in each suit.

4 The numbers go from 1–9.

5 North, East, West, and South, four of each.

6 F means Flower.

7 Eight Flowers.

8 Words and numbers on the Flowers mean nothing.

9 "Soap" is the White Dragon.

10 Jokers can never be part of a Pair, or a Single.

11 The 1 Bam usually is a bird.

12 The Red Dragon goes with the Craks, the Green with Bams, and the White with Dots.

13 Winds, Flowers and Jokers are neutral, and unrelated to the Dots, Bams and Craks.

14 Soaps are neutral when they stand in for Zeros in year hands: 2021, 2022, etc.

Chapter 3

Building the Walls and Dealing the Tiles

There are five ways players get tiles during the game. These are: the **deal**, the **Charleston** (the tile exchange that goes on after the deal), **picking** a tile from the **wall, calling** for a **discard**, and **exchanging** a tile to get a Joker. In this chapter you'll learn how you get the tiles you begin with, i.e., "the hand you are dealt." Many aspects of mahjong around the world are the same, but the NMJL's version of the game, aka Mah Jongg, has some unique aspects.

Mixing the Tiles

You all know from playing cards that the deck has to be shuffled—otherwise people could cheat or gain some other unfair advantage. It's the same with Mah Jongg—but you can't shuffle tiles. These tiles are mixed the way they have been for almost two hundred years: on the table. Players carefully turn all the tiles face down, and then move them all around with their hands, ensuring tiles are getting properly mixed. This is called "**washing** the tiles." In the early years of the game, and still at times today, this was an opportunity for ladies to show off rings, bracelets, and manicures. And now that men have rejoined the ranks, they get to show off, too. Cufflinks and big watches are part of the "oohs" and "ahhs" portion of the game.

Many of us experienced players have seen people slide Cards (or stiff plastic) under the tiles to "mix them well," flipping the pieces in the air. This is not the way to do things in MJ. Tiles can crack, break, chip or go missing. You don't want that to happen to a new set of tiles, and thinking about this happening with an antique or vintage set is much too upsetting. Encourage others to keep to the great tradition of nice, gentle movements of the tiles around the table.

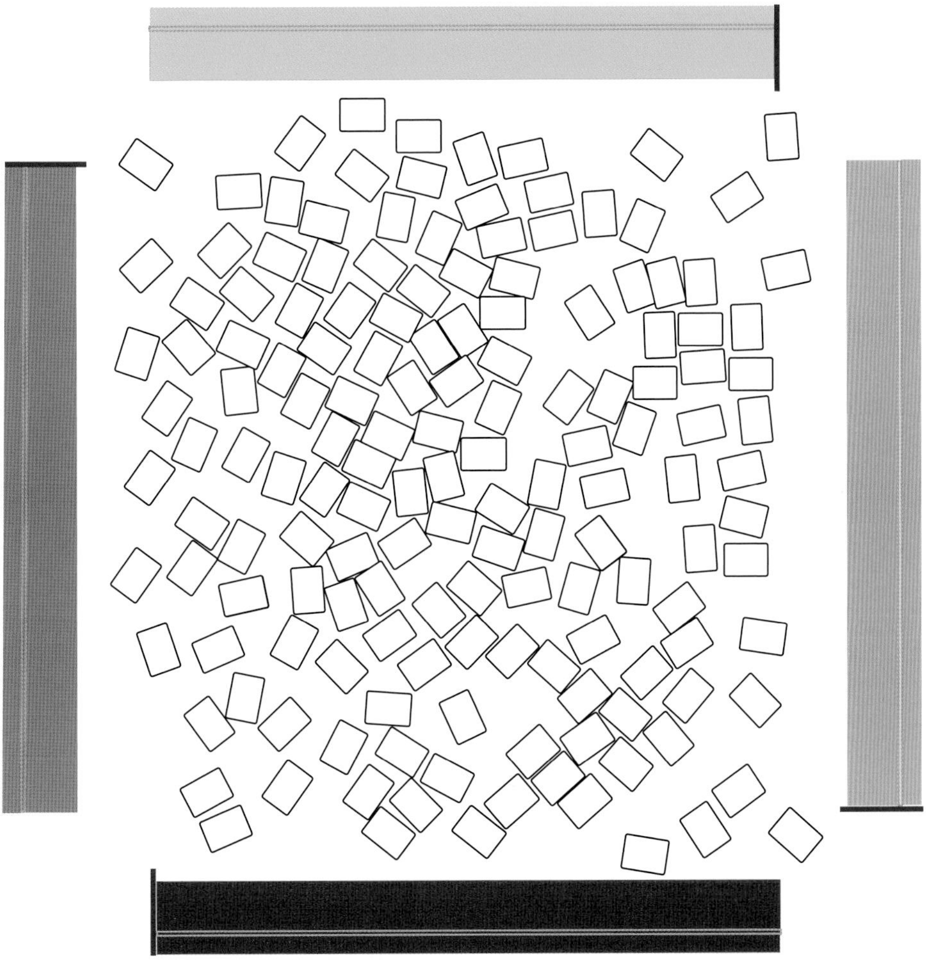

All tiles are mixed facedown on the table.

Once you've spent a while mixing the tiles (this is one of the times Mah Jongg conversation is at its best), it's time to build the walls.

Building the Walls

Mah Jongg has its origins in China, and when people think of China, they often think of the Great Wall. So of course there have to be **walls** in mahjong, in every style of play. Players build walls, and take tiles from walls when it's their turn to play.

Although in China people don't use **racks**, in the NMJL style of play, we love them. All four players have a rack, placed horizontally in front of them. The rack serves three purposes: when **building** the walls, tiles are placed in front of each rack (tiles will be dealt and drawn from these walls); the slanted back part of the rack is where players have their own tiles (hidden from the other players); and the flat top of the rack is where **exposures** go. (More about that later.) Because the only thing certain in the game of Mah Jongg is that nothing is certain, there is not a definite relationship between the length of the rack and the number of tiles placed in front of it. The rack might be any length and the tiles any size, therefore there's no standard for where your wall might end.

In Mah Jongg, the "wall" is the lineup of facedown tiles, two tiles high, in front of each rack. On the far left of most racks is a **stopper**, a piece of plastic or metal that protrudes from the front of the rack. Start your wall there: butt your tiles against it and build. You'll make a two-tiered row, 19 tiles long. At first you'll want to count your tiles to make sure you have two layers of 19, i.e., 38 tiles. But soon you'll realize you don't really have to count: you can quickly see which walls are too short or too long.

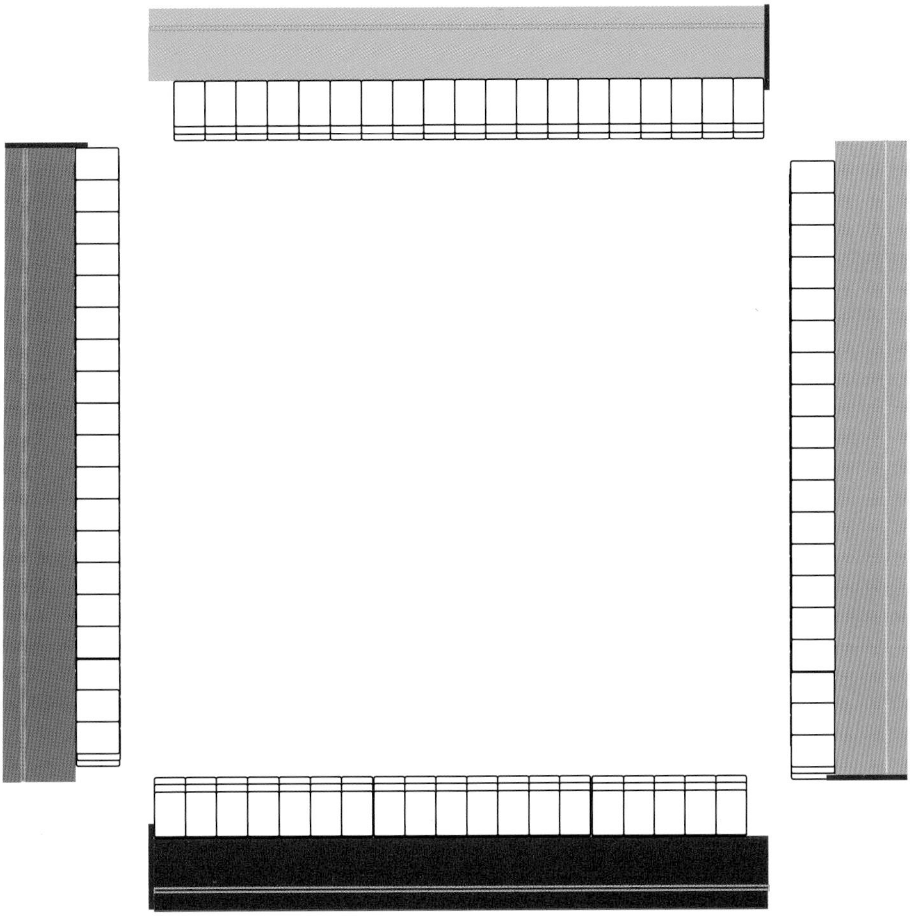

Four tile walls are built, 19 tiles long and two tiles high.
Each player will have a total of 38 tiles in front of the rack.

G&T Time:

Gregg: I like to count the tiles in my walls. For me there's something quite soothing in the wall "building and counting" rituals—it's a bit like the calm before the storm (when the actual game begins). A lot of us like this part of play.

Toby: I like to do things quickly, to get in the maximum number of games. I say: "Don't count your tiles!" When everyone has made his or her walls, look. You'll see who needs tiles. Counting takes too long!

Dealing the Tiles

Once everyone has equal walls in front of their racks, it's time to pick tiles. But of course there are **rituals** associated with this, too. Play starts by throwing two dice. When you're the host or hostess, you'll be **East** (the **dealer**) first. This means you'll start dividing the tiles, or dealing. If you're in a neutral place, like a café or park, each player will roll the dice, and the person who rolls the highest number will be East. Sometimes two or even three people will have the same high number. Keep throwing until one person has the highest number. (We call this a "dice off!")

When you know who's East, the other players have the following Wind positions:

WEST

SOUTH NORTH

EAST

Say you're East: throw the dice to determine where to **break** the wall. This helps to randomize where the deal starts, minimizing the possibility of cheating. Everyone gets to be East, in a counter-clockwise rotation, from the first dealer.

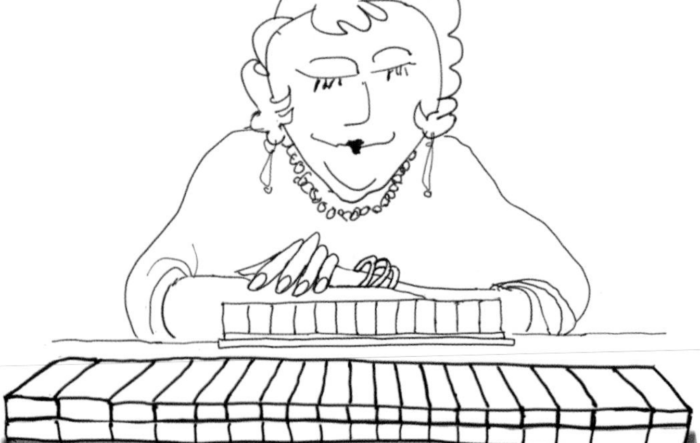

The Great Wall of Ina.

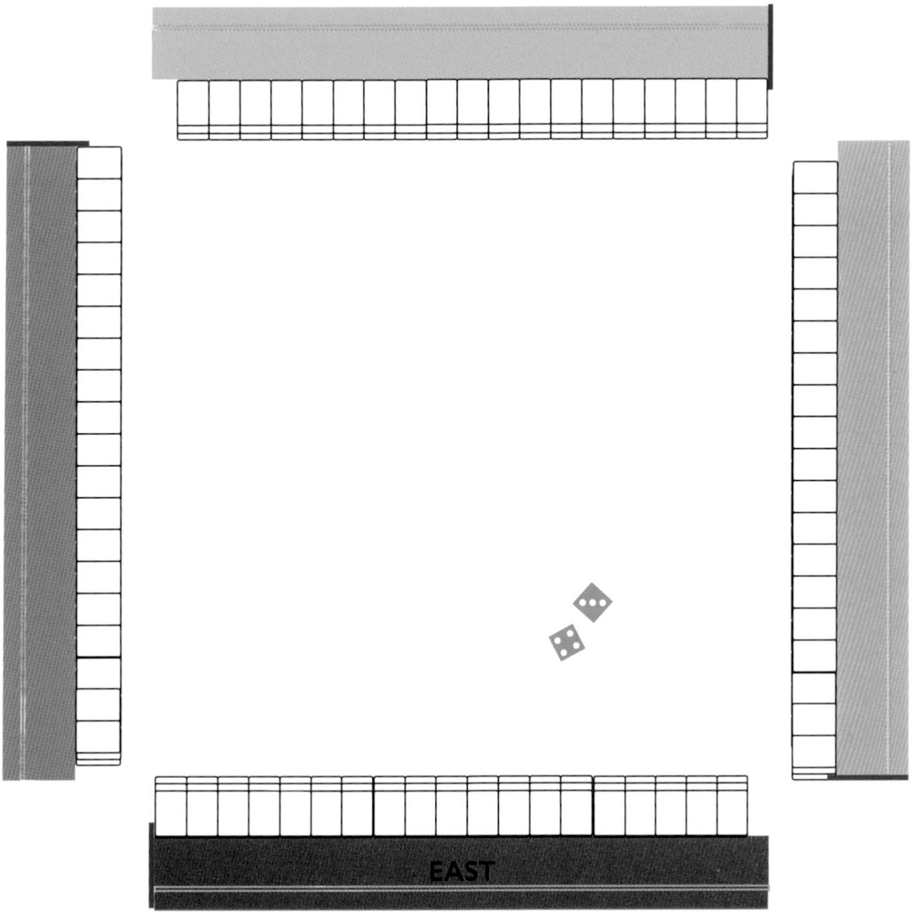

Once it's determined who's East (here, the player with the red rack),
East throws again, here a 7.

The first thing to do after rolling the dice is to move them to East's right (orange), indicating who'll be East the next round. East pushes the wall in front of him or her out diagonally into the table, with the far right edge of the wall toward the table's center. Players might use their racks to push the wall out. Some racks have attached "**pushers**" (flat pieces anchored to part of the rack that help guide the wall where it should go).

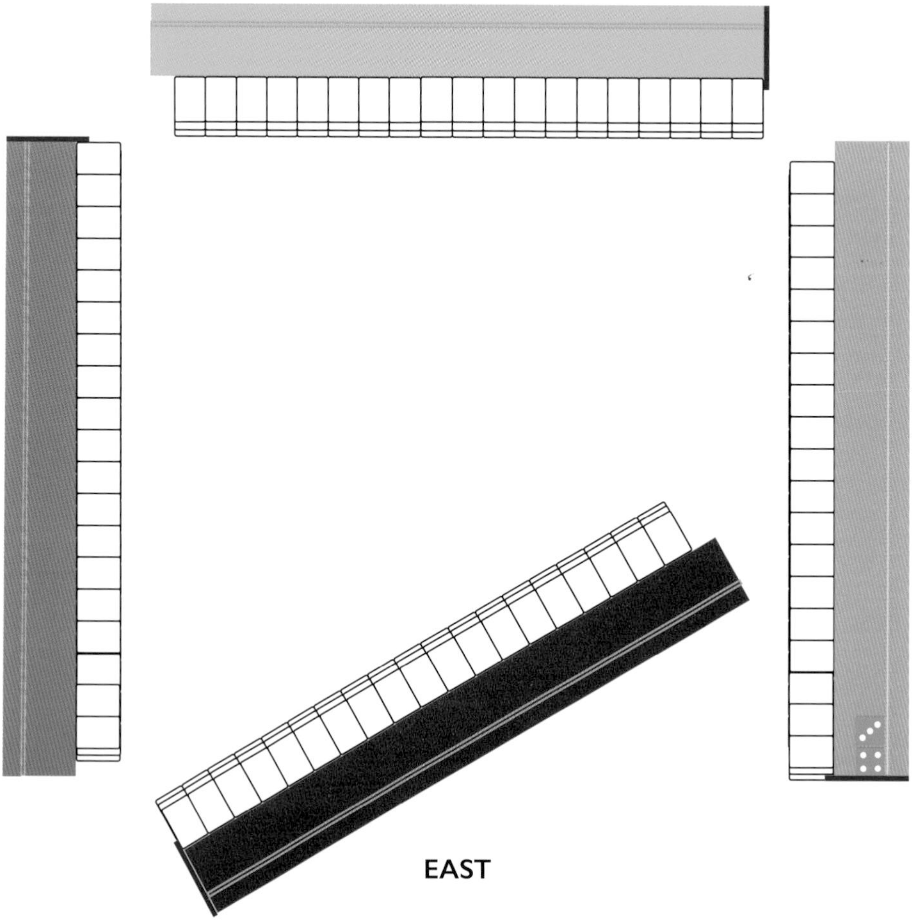

Dice are placed, face-up showing the number thrown, on top of the rack to East's right, orange. East's wall is pushed out, with the right-most edge of the wall toward the middle of the table.

We like to place the dice on the top of the rack of the next East, face up showing the numbers thrown. Some players pay out double if doubles were thrown on the dice, so a pair of threes will have a different payout than a four and a two.

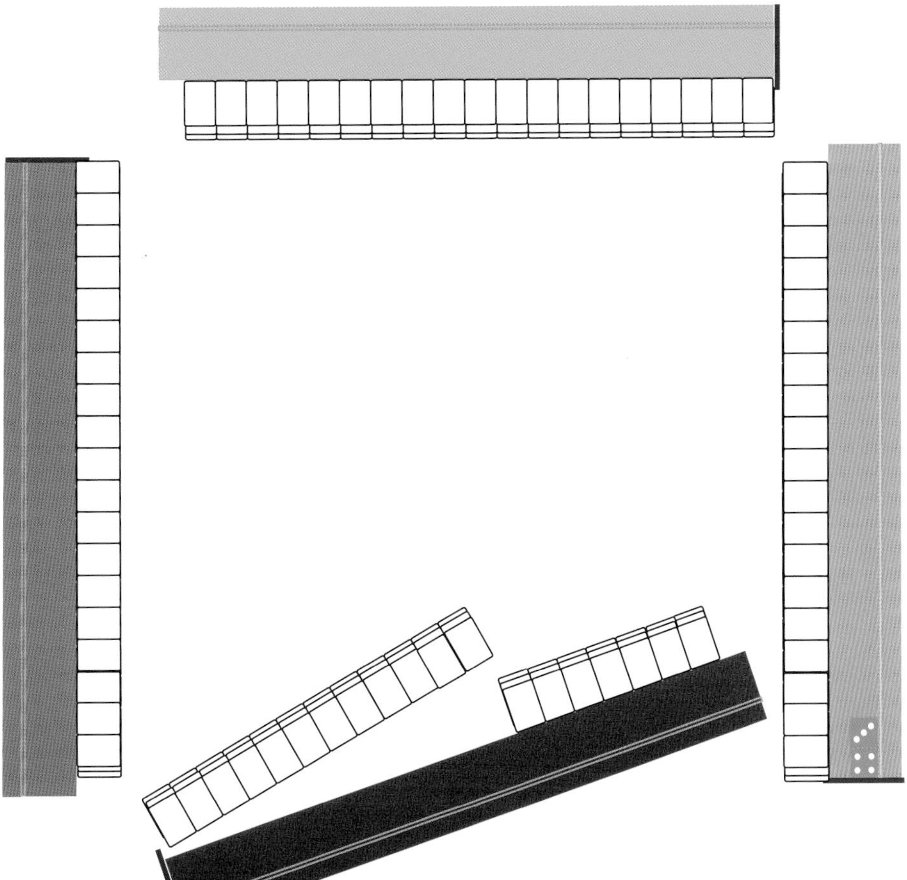

Take two layers of seven tiles (7 was the number thrown on the dice)
for a total of 14 tiles, counting from the right end of the wall.

From the right of East's wall, count off the number of tile **stacks** from right to left, according to what was rolled on the dice. When you get to the number thrown, that is where you'll break the wall.

The tiles to the right of the break are what you, as East, pull back toward you. Place them in front of your rack. This is the "**Hot Wall**." These tiles will be the last ones played with, if the game is not won before then. The other tiles—those to the left of the break—are where the dealing will start.

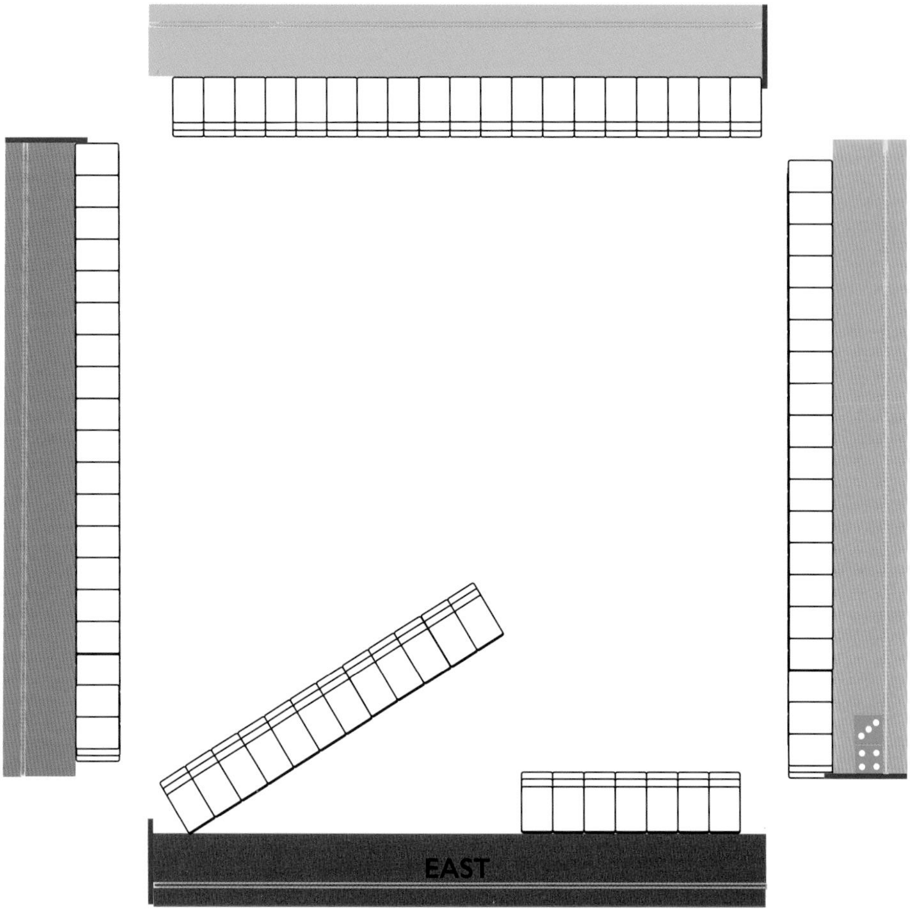

Those seven pairs are brought back and kept along East's wall, becoming the "Hot Wall."
East can easily be identified: a short wall in front of the player.

In Mah Jongg each person usually takes his or her own tiles (although sometimes East deals to everyone, a bit like a tea party with the hostess pouring the tea!). Although players usually help themselves to tiles, this is the "deal." Tiles are always taken from the centermost portion of the wall.

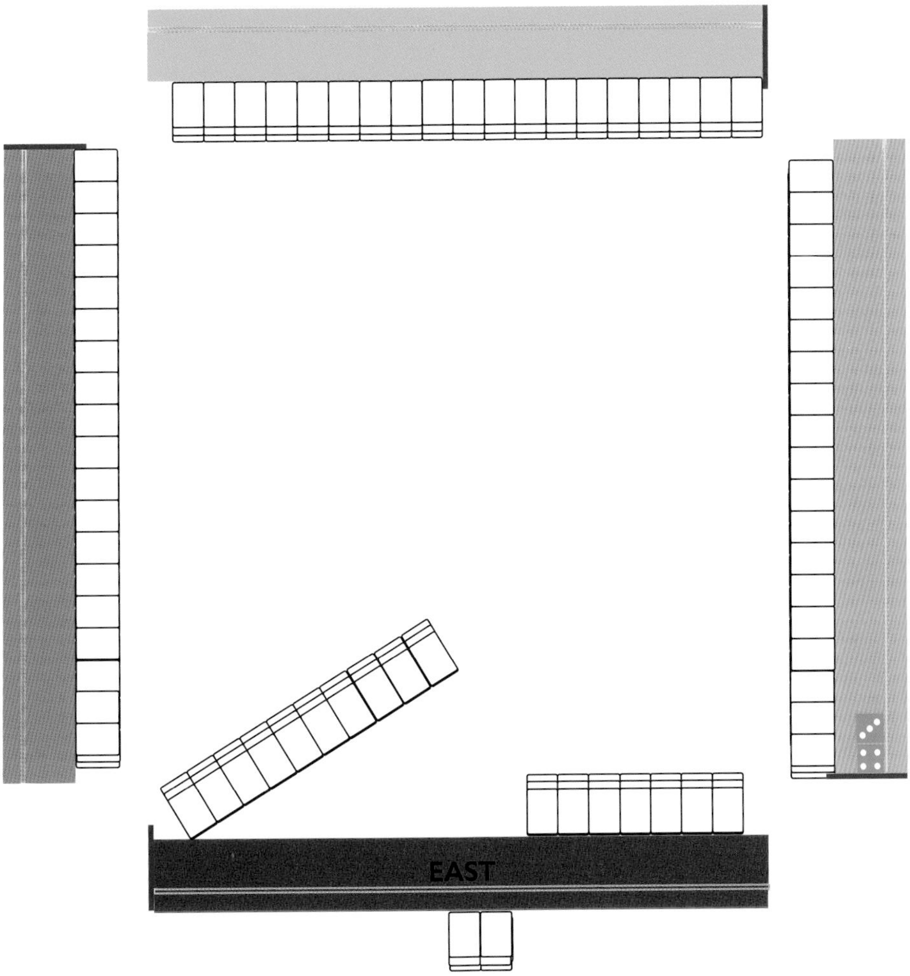

East takes the first two stacks of tiles (four tiles) and puts them behind the rack.
These will be East's tiles.

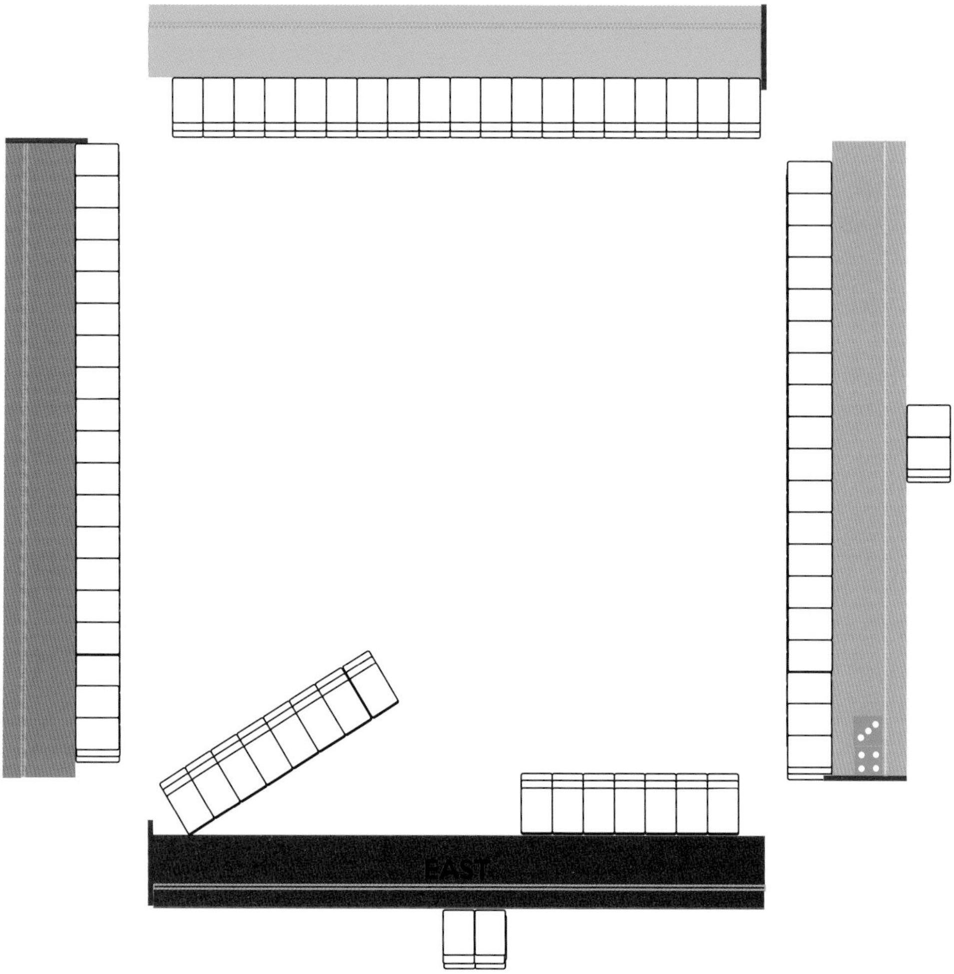

Players take their two stacks (four tiles) in a counter-clockwise manner.
The player to East's right is the next to take tiles.

The player to East's right takes the next two stacks of tiles.

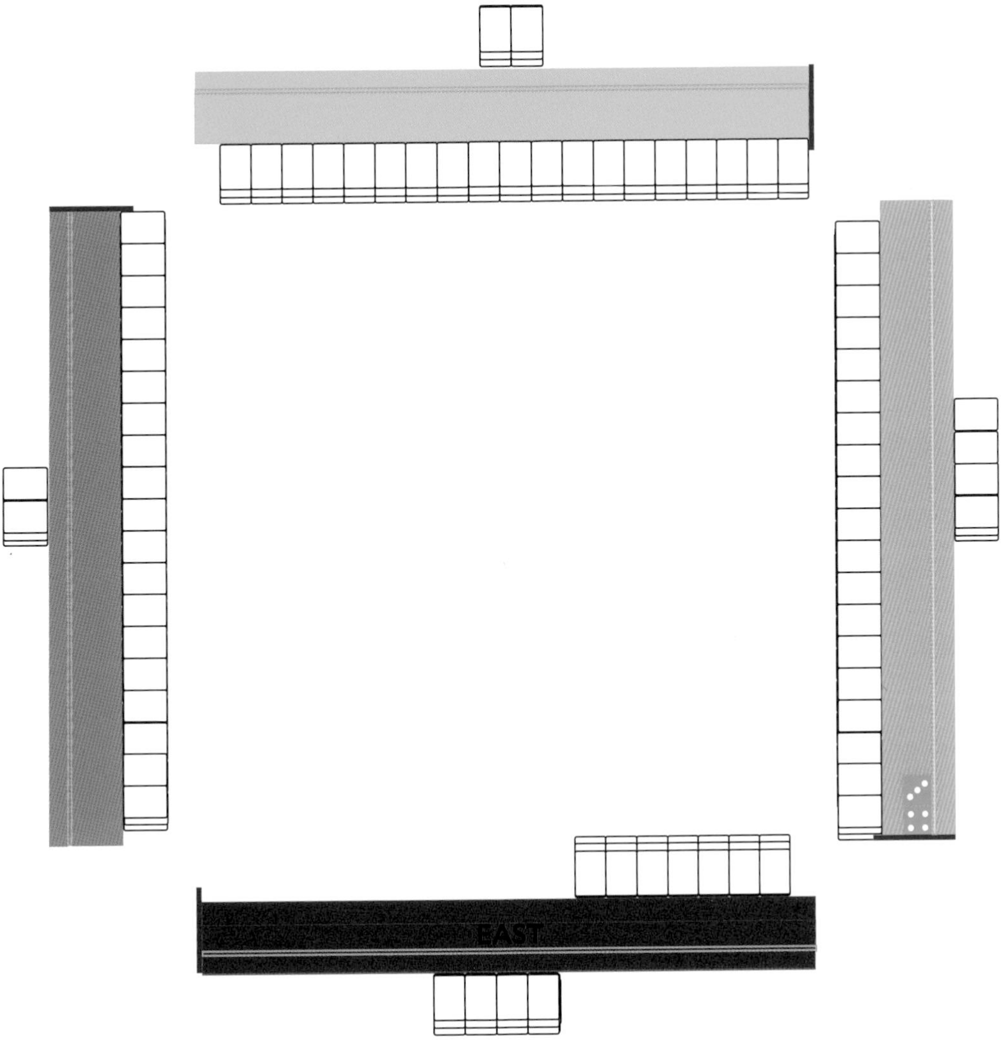

Players take their tiles until there are no more tiles in the wall.

Players go around the table counterclockwise (Right is Right), taking two stacks of two tiles at a time; in other words, four tiles each turn.

Of course, in mahjong there's always a quirk ("exceptions are the norm"). There will soon be a time when either no tiles are left or only one stack remains, not enough for the players to get their tiles.

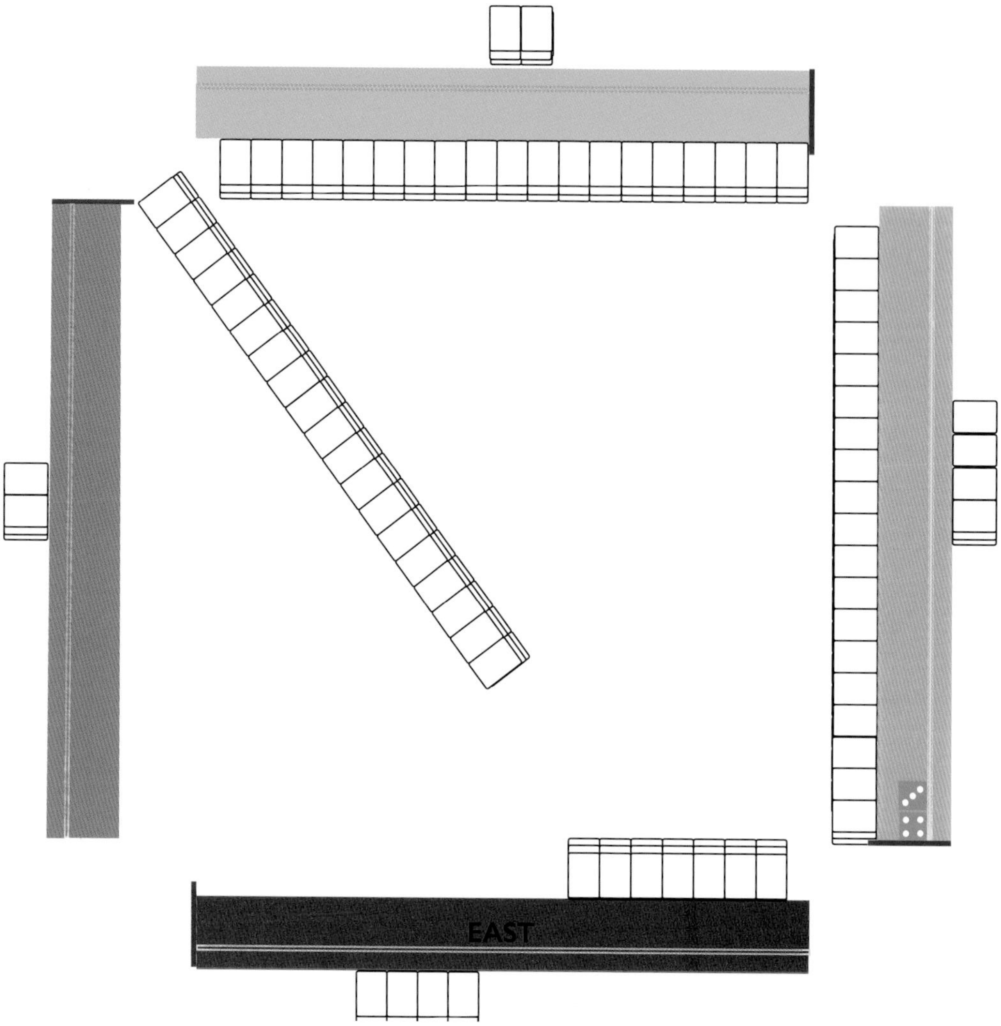

The wall to the left of East is pushed out, with the right-most edge of the wall toward the center of the table.

If one stack remains, those two tiles will be taken along with the next two tiles from the new wall clockwise from, or to the left of, the first wall. That wall will be pushed out, with the rightmost corner toward the middle of the table.

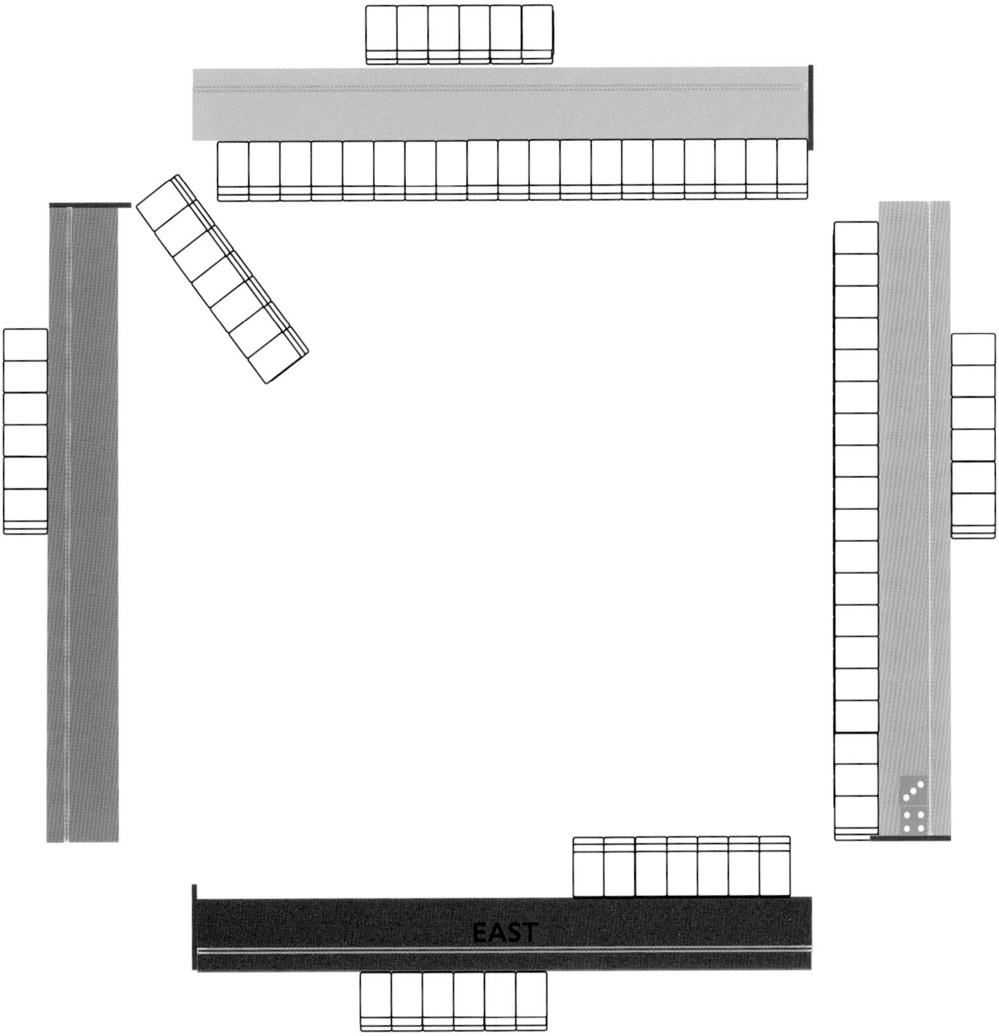

Players continue taking two stacks of tiles until everyone has six stacks (12 tiles).

Taking the tiles continues until all players have three stacks of four tiles, in other words, 12 tiles. When getting tiles, put them in front of yourself, giving everyone a visual cue as to where you are in the "deal" of the tiles.

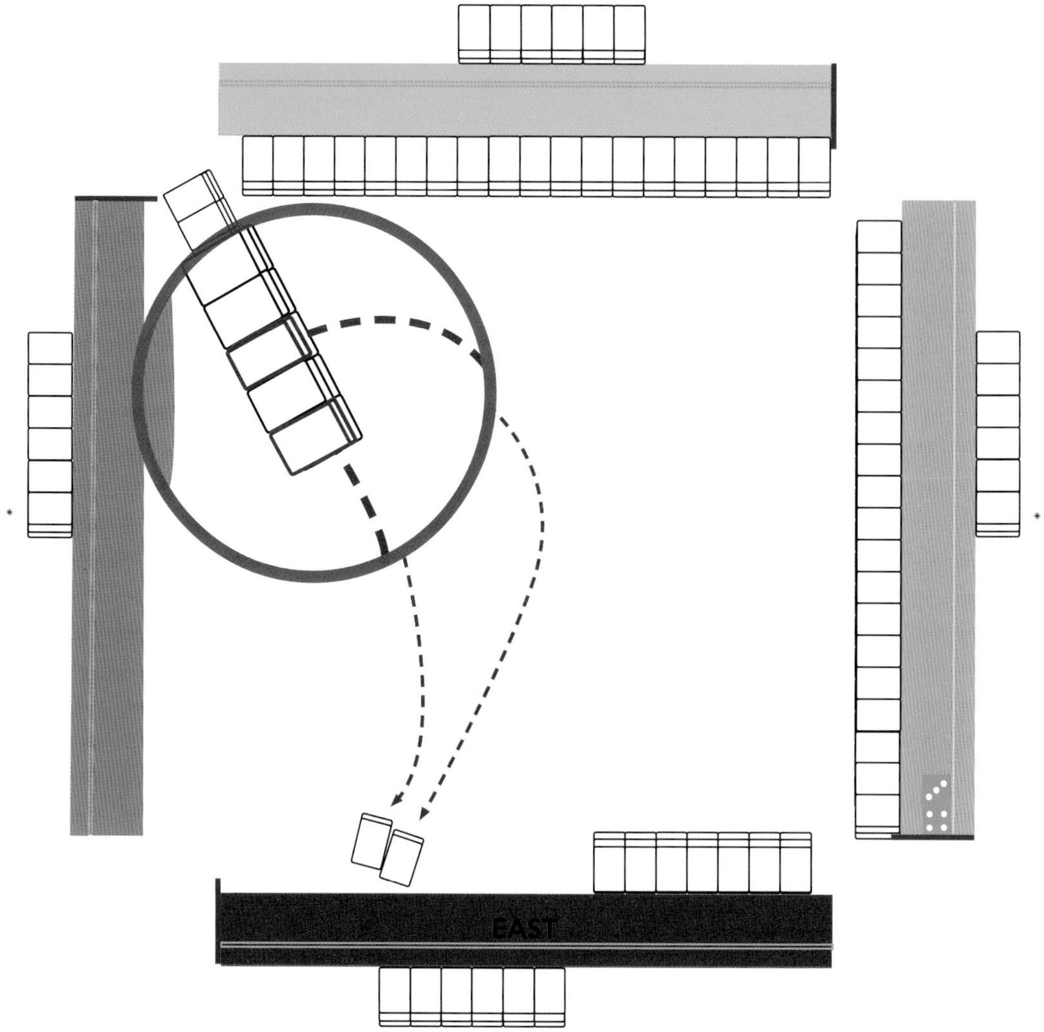

East always has an advantage: 14 tiles. East takes the top tile from the first and the third stacks of the wall.

Now that everyone has 12 tiles, there's another dealing "wrinkle": East will now take the top first and third tiles from the wall from the right and place them with his or her group.

> Everything in Mah Jongg is on the right, from the right and to the right, except for the person who pushes out their wall next. Right is Right, but walls open to the left—in other words, clockwise! If it's about people, it's to the right. If it's about the wall, it's left. This does take time to wrap your head around (it seems like torture to all of us), but you'll get it.

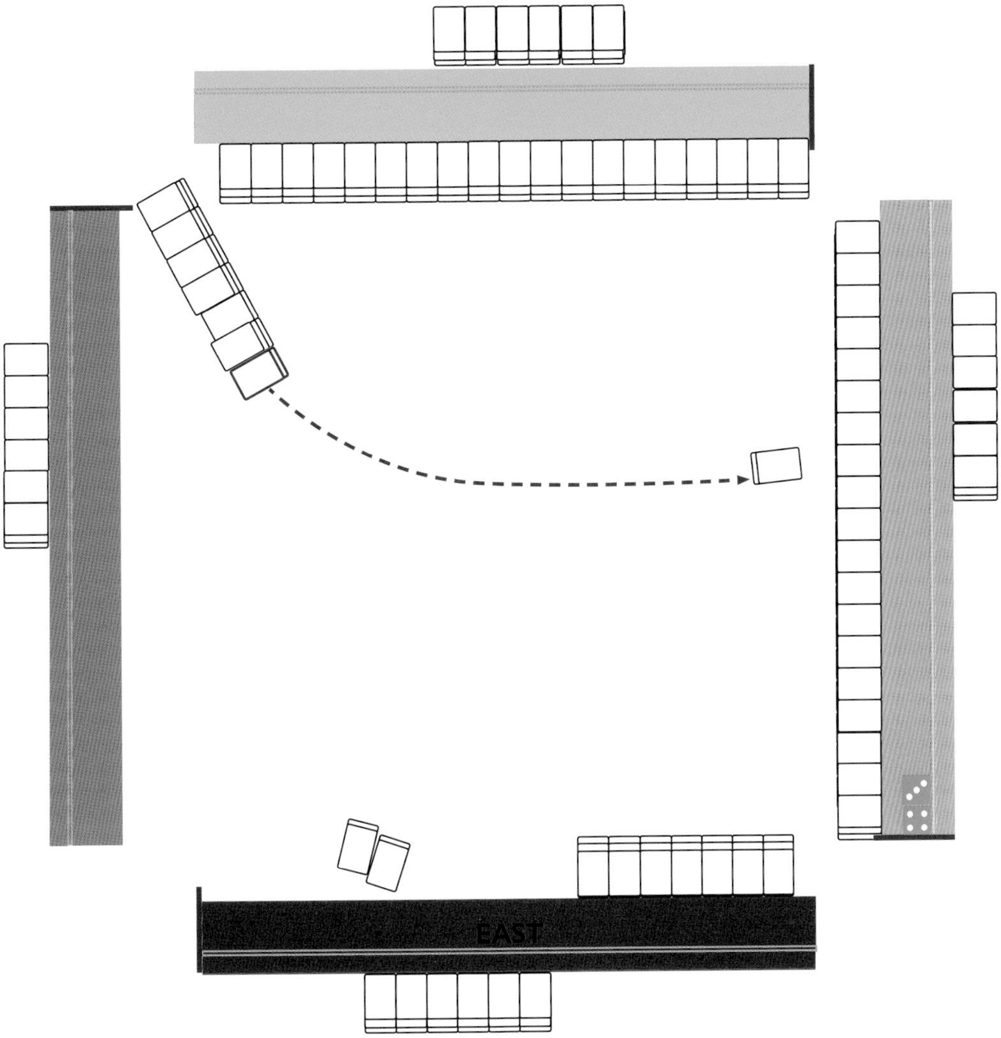

Orange takes the bottom tile from the stack.

Next, the player to their right (orange) will take one tile (the near lower tile).

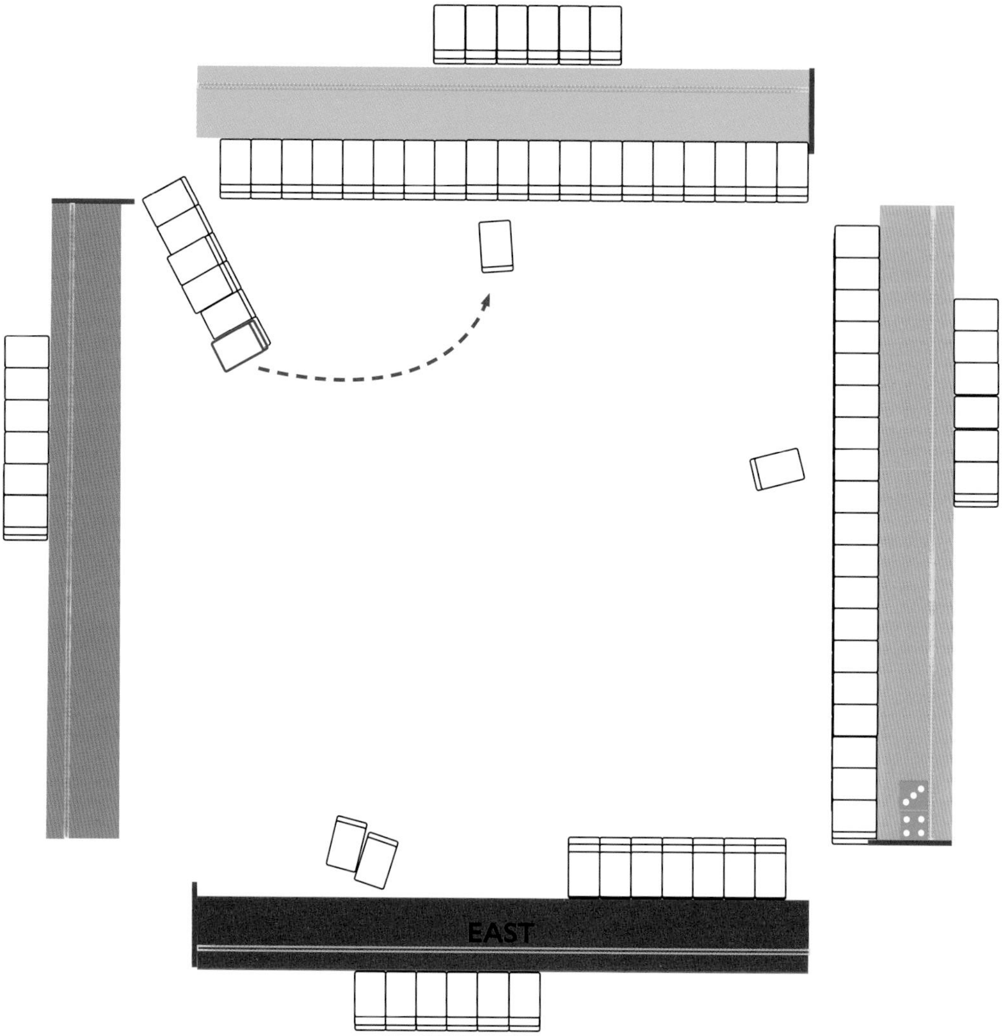

Blue takes the top tile from the remaining stack.

The player to *their* right (blue) will take a tile (the top next tile).

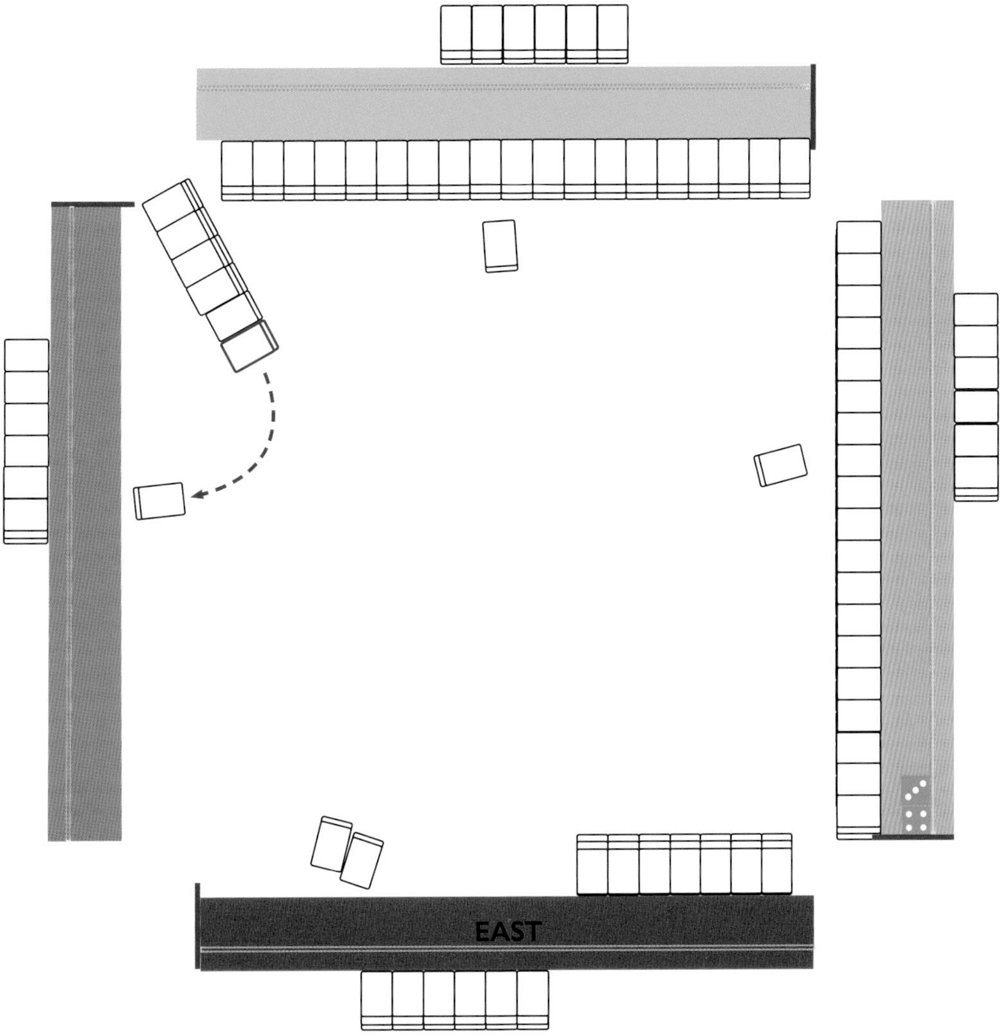

Purple takes the remaining lower tile of that stack.

Finally, the last player (purple) will take one tile (the near lower tile). All tiles must be taken from the centermost end of the wall. East will have 14 tiles, and all other players 13.

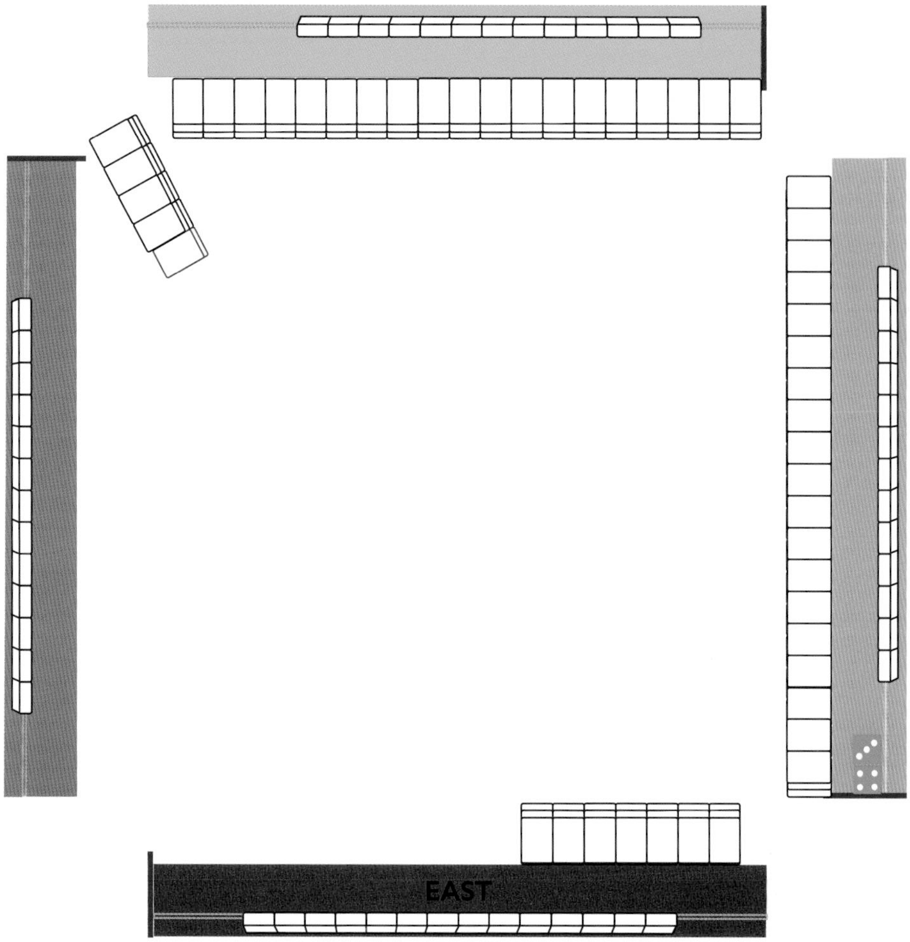

One lower tile remains in the wall. Players arrange their tiles on the inner ledge of the rack.

The wall will be left with one tile of the right-most stack. This tile will be the first one picked when the game begins.

Once you have your tiles, start racking. This means you'll each place your tiles on the lip of the rack facing you, hidden from other players. The tiles that remain in the wall will be the first tiles picked in the game.

Interestingly, although we don't really want to think about it, East has an advantage: 14 tiles instead of 13. East is the only one who can yell out "Mah Jongg" before play begins and don't we all want that to happen for us!

One last hint. If you're playing with a set you have never seen before, it is perfectly fine and even preferable to ask to see certain tiles before building your wall. Players often ask to see the One Bam, the Dragons, the Flowers, and the Jokers. These can vary so much from set to set, especially with vintage ones. You don't want to find yourself in the middle of a game puzzling over which tile you have in your hand.

Summary

Players mix tiles face down on the table (washing the tiles). Then walls are built in front of each rack, two tiles high, 19 tiles long. Dice are thrown by each player to determine East—the player with the highest number. East throws the dice again to determine where the wall will be broken, akin to cutting a deck of cards. East's wall is pushed out into the middle of the table, right-most end toward the middle. From the right edge of the wall, East counts the number, seen on the dice, of tile stacks. These are moved back to East's rack and will not be dealt. They become the "Hot Wall," the last tiles played in the game, if needed. From the now-shortened wall, East takes the first two stacks of tiles (four tiles) at a time, then the other players follow suit, in a counter-clockwise direction. When the wall either has one stack of tiles left, or no stacks, the next wall to the left of East (purple) gets pushed out, once again with the right-most edge toward the middle of the table. (It might happen that a player takes one stack from one wall and one from another.) Players continue to take tiles until everyone has six stacks (12 tiles). East then takes the top first and third tile from the wall, orange the bottom closest tile, blue the next top tile, and purple the bottom closest tile. All players now have 13 tiles, but East has a slight advantage with 14.

Quiz

1 How does someone become East?

2 Why are the dice thrown again after we know who is East?

3 What end of East's wall do we count from to break the wall?

4 What is done with those far right tiles that we counted off from the dice throw?

5 What end of the wall goes toward the center of the table?

6 What happens if there is only one stack of tiles left for the deal in a wall, and the player needs two stacks?

7 Which player pushes out their wall when the tiles are used up in a wall?

8 What is a stopper?

9 How do you know who will be East in the next game?

10 How many tiles constitute a wall?

11 Who takes the first and third tiles at the end?

12 Should you wait until everyone has all their tiles to start arranging yours?

Answers

1 The host or hostess, or the player with the highest number rolled on the dice.

2 The dice are thrown to find out where the wall will be "cut."

3 We count from the far right of East's wall to see where the wall is broken. Each number on the dice indicates a stack of tiles.

4 The tiles brought back become the Hot Wall, the last tiles played in the game.

5 The right end of the wall is closest to the center of the table.

6 The person to the left swings out their wall and the player takes from there.

7 The player on the left of the empty wall is next to push out their wall.

8 The end piece on a rack that nests the tiles in place.

9 The player to the right of the last East is the next East.

10 Each wall is 19 tiles across (stacked two high, thus 38 tiles).

11 The dealer, who is also East. Both answers are correct!

12 Yes, rack when all players have their 13 or 14 tiles.

Chapter 4

The Card and How to Use It

The **National Mah Jongg League (NMJL)** has been the standard for American Mah Jongg since 1937. The **League** has a unique approach to the game with its rules, rituals, and even number and kinds of tiles. Like other versions of mahjong, the goal is to put together a combination of 14 tiles, a **hand**, but the NMJL dictates the ways the tiles can be assembled. Whoever completes one of their hands first is the winner, happily calling "Mah Jongg!" Every April the League issues a new Card, **the Card**, with different combinations, showing the latest groupings of tiles, the hands, required to win the game. Other than these changes, everything usually is the same: the tiles, the rules and play. Given the League's Card is copyrighted and pertains to the year it's printed, for purposes of this book we're providing you with our own timeless version, **our Card**. By using our Card, you'll grasp all the concepts you need. (When we write **card** with a lower case "c" the statement applies to both cards.) The Card has different colors, categories, and hands with important details in parentheses. You must be familiar with all these to be a good player. There are abbreviations you need to know: **F** is Flower, **D** is Dragon, **NEWS** is North, East, West and South, and the number "**0**" is a White Dragon, aka Soap.

The Card

When you become comfortable with the types of hands and the other important directions associated with them on our Card, you can easily understand the NMJL one. We'll start by looking at the inside of the card, where the tile combinations appear.

DO THIS

Remove our Card from the back of the book. You'll need to cut it out and tape it together properly. It's in the form of a compact trifold, so you'll be able carry it around easily.

The Colors

You'll first notice there are three colors: black (dark blue on the NMJL one), green and red. The colors do not indicate specific suits**.** Green doesn't mean **Bams**, Red doesn't mean **Craks.** Each color represents any suit, and when the color changes, you must change the suit. If a line—a hand—has one color, use any suit. If a hand has two colors, use any two suits. If a hand has three colors, you must use all three suits. Remember Flowers, Winds and Zeros are neutral, so even if they're the same color as the numbers you're working with, this doesn't matter: Winds, Flowers and "0"s (Zeros) go with everything. If there's a D (Dragon) the same color as a number, that means they have to be the same suit; a different color means a different suit.

The Categories

There are **Categories** or **Sections**, the "named" areas of the card. Categories are separated by extra space or by the trifold crease, and remain the same every year, with two exceptions. The bottom left is often an "Addition" hand (but it can be another mathematical operation). The year section, top left, changes as well. (On our Card we've created a timeless Century version.) Each line represents a hand.

The Parentheses

Notice that most hands have something in the parentheses on the same line. These explanations help you better understand what's needed. They'll let you know if you're allowed any flexibility in the hand. You must read and understand it. The parenthetical gives you restrictions and opportunities. Some of the card is like the game Simon Says: you're simply copying what you see. But there is some freedom as seen in the parentheses.

Sometimes words are abbreviated. The most frequent one is Number, abbreviated "**No.**" if just for one number, or "**Nos**." for several numbers. Pair may be **Pr**; **Consec** is short for Consecutive. **Kong** is four of a kind, and **Pung** is three of a kind.

Getting to Know Our Card

We're going to jump around a bit, starting with the easiest areas, working our way toward the harder ones. You probably should think about them when you start to play the game, too. We'll start with Like Numbers, on the left. Just remember, with the exceptions of Singles and Pairs, Jokers can make up for what you don't have.

Like Numbers

"Like" on the Card means same. In this section the NMJL gives you the freedom to choose any number for your hand, but it must be the same number in all suits. If you have several of the same number, this is a good place to be. You can use all 1s, as seen on the Card, but you can do any number you have a lot of: (e.g., 2s, 7s, 9s, or whatever). If you have a few of one number in two or three suits this would be a good area to work on.

Line 1: FF 1111 1111 1111 (Any Like Nos.)

You can use any of the same numbers.

Like Numbers, all 1s

DO THIS

Get a Pair of Flowers and make this hand using 1s. Make it with 9s. Have a couple of Jokers and use them for numbers when you can. Of course, you can't use them for the Flowers because they're a pair. (Jokers are never part of a pair).

You can make the hand with 1s, but also all 2s, 3s and so on. Choose any number you like to make this hand as long as the numbers are the same, and you've used three suits.

Line 2: 11 DD 111 DDD 1111 (3 suits; Any Like Nos.)

If you have some of the same numbers and Dragons, this would be a good hand to choose. You must use all three suits (there are three colors) but any same numbers. Remember: the color does not indicate a particular suit. You'll need a pair of numbers and that suit's matching Dragons, Pungs of the same number in another suit and its matching Dragons, and a Kong of the third suit. The only place you can't use Jokers are for the Pairs.

DO THIS

Instead of using 1s, do 4s. Get Pairs of **4 Bams** and **Green Dragons**, Pungs of 4 Dots and Soaps, and a Kong of **4 Craks**. Try it with other numbers, too. This hand will help you become more comfortable with which Dragons go with which suit, and where you can use Jokers.

Quints

The Quint (five tiles) hands, found on the middle section, are unusual as they require Jokers. There are four of every tile with the exception of Flowers and Jokers. Well, in order to make a grouping of five, you'll usually use Jokers. If you are lucky enough to be dealt a few Jokers, you might just consider these hands.

Line 1: 22 333 4444 55555 (1 suit; These Nos. only)

You must use these numbers, but you can pick the suit. There are five 5s on our Card, and you have to use at least one Joker to make that set.

Line 3: FFFF NNNNN 11111 (Any Wind; Any No.)

For the Kong of Flowers you don't need Jokers, but you do for the Quints of Wind and the number. Reading the parentheses you'll see it can be any Wind and number. Using at least one Joker in the second two groupings, you must have five (Quints) of any Wind and any number in any suit. You decide which Wind and number are your strongest.

DO THIS

Use Souths and **2 Craks**.

FFFF SSJSS 2C 2C J 2C 2C

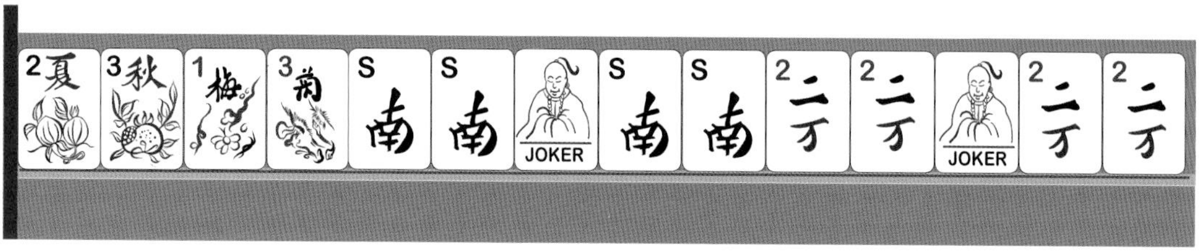

Quints of Souths and 2 Craks

Use your Flowers, West Winds and **7 Bams** (and of course two Jokers), and make this hand:

FFFF WWJWW 7B 7B J 7B 7B

Try another of your own choosing. Pick your favorite Wind and number and give it a whirl.

Consecutive Run

This group usually has the most flexibility, except for the top line.

Line 1: 11 222 3333 444 55 or 55 666 7777 888 99 (Any 1 Suit)

It must be played with one suit, numbers ranging from 1–5 or 5–9. Pick any suit, but the numbers must be these numbers. We used Bams.

DO THIS

Pick one suit and make both versions of the hand, the low run (1–5) and the high one (5–9). Use two Jokers where you can (not in the Pairs).

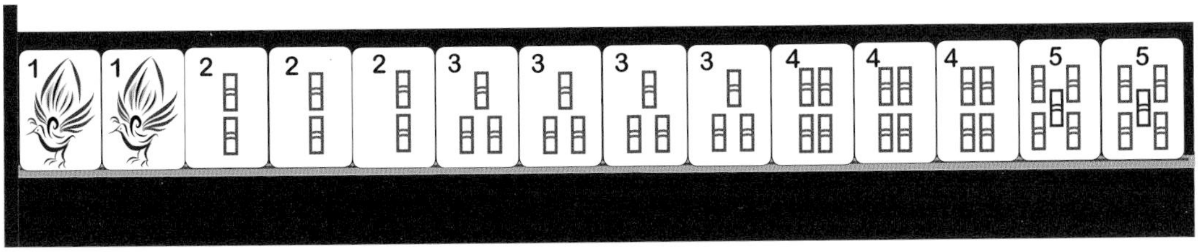

Low consecutive run

Line 2: 111 2222 333 4444 (Any 2 Suits; 4 Consecutive Nos.)

There's freedom here. You can use 1 2 3 and 4, but it's any run of four numbers. You're free to use any four consecutive numbers, but you must pay attention to how the suits are described: the first two groups are one suit (one color), and the next two, another (a different color).

DO THIS

Build this hand with two suits and two Jokers. (All the groupings are Pungs and Kongs, so Jokers can go anywhere.) Start with **5 Bams** and **6 Bams**, then switch to **Craks** for the last two groups. Make a hand with 3 Dots and 4 Dots and choose a different suit for the next two numbers. Just remember: you can use Craks, Bams or Dots for the first two groups and Craks, Bams or Dots for the second group as long as you use two suits. Two colors = two suits. You can start your run with any number up to 6. Your combinations are: 111 2222 333 4444, 222 3333 444 5555, 333 4444 555 6666, 444 5555 666 7777, 555 6666 777 8888, and 666 7777 888 9999.

Line 3: FFFF 1111 2222 DD or FFFF 1111 2222 DD (1 or 3 suits)

You have a bit of freedom here: one or three suits. Say you work on the hand needing three suits: you need four Flowers, any two consecutive numbers in different suits and un-matching Dragons, i.e., Dragons that don't go with either of the suits you are using.

DO THIS

Make this using Kongs of Flowers. If you have Kongs of 6 Dots and 7 Craks, which Dragons would you need? The Greens. Use two Jokers where you can, but not for the Dragons. (You remember the rule about pairs by now.) Make it again with one suit, the Dots, starting with any number 1–8. What Dragons will you use? The Soaps.

Line 5: 1111 22 22 22 3333 (Any 3 Consecutive Nos.; Pairs Middle Nos. Only)

This type of hand appears with great frequency. It's often called the "**Sandwich Hand**," because Pairs of middle numbers are nestled between two Kongs. You need to have Pairs of the middle numbers, "the sandwich filling," but you can use Jokers for any missing numbers in the Kongs. This hand can start with 1, as seen here, but you can start with anything up to 7 as the lowest number.

DO THIS

Make this hand using Kongs of 4s and 6s, and complete it using all three Pairs of 5s in the three different suits. Now try another.

13579

This section is also called the "**Odds**," because it's only Odd numbers. Here you must conform to the numbers on the card.

Line 1: 11 333 5555 777 99 (1 Suit)

The only freedom you have is the suit you choose. The 1s and 9s can't have Jokers.

DO THIS

Pick a suit and make this hand. It's not that different from the first line of the Consecutive Number area. You see one color, so it's one suit.

All odd Craks

Line 2: 111 3333 333 5555 or 555 7777 777 9999 (2 Suits)

This line is not that different than the second line of Consecutive Numbers. The first sets of numbers must be from one suit, and the second sets from another, but you get to pick which.

Line 3: FFFF 1111 33 5555 or FFFF 1111 33 5555 (1 or 3 suits)

You have a choice: the one or three suit approach. For three suits, along with the four Flowers you can possibly use: Kongs of 1 Dots, a Pair of **3 Bams** and a Kong of **5 Craks**. You might want **1 Bams**, a Pair of **3 Craks** and a Kong of 5 Dots, and so on… <u>you</u> decide. Where can't you use Jokers? You know: in the Pair! (You've got this: no more reminders.)

DO THIS

Make this hand using just one suit, and two Jokers. Then make it using all three suits, and two Jokers.

Line 7: 111 3 555 555 7 999 (2 Suits)

You can use <u>any</u> one suit for the first set of numbers 1–5 and <u>any</u> other suit for the second numbers 5–9. You just have to have two suits and those pesky Singles: the 3 and the 7. Remember: no Jokers for Singles either.

Winds and Dragons

In this section, you <u>must copy</u> the Winds. If you see an N on the card, you must use a North. This is different from the Quints. The Dragons, however, often are your choice.

Line 2: FF DDDD NEWS DDDD (Dragons Any 2 Suits)

You need two Flowers, and two Kongs of Dragons, but you can use any two; we used Reds and Greens. There's a grouping of NEWS: you <u>must</u> use North, East, West and South. (No Jokers can substitute for single tiles.)

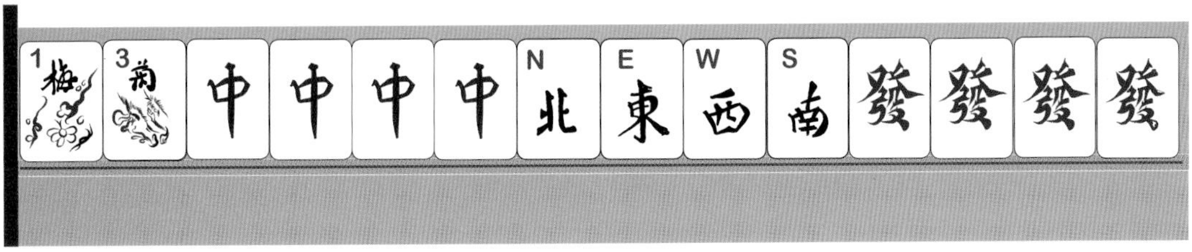

NEWS with Reds and Greens

Line 3: NNNN SSSS 111 111 (2 Suits, Pungs Odd Numbers Only)

Norths and Souths typically go with the Odd numbers. (Hint: both North and South have an odd number of letters.) You can pick any Odd numbers you like, just so that the numbers are the same in two different suits, but your Winds are Norths and Souths.

Line 4: EEEE WWWW 222 222 (2 Suits, Even Nos. Only)

Easts and Wests tend to be associated with Even numbers. E is for East and E is for Even—got it? (And both East and West have even numbers of letters—even better!) Your Winds can only be Easts and Wests. Use any even numbers here as long as they're the same. Pungs of **2 Bams** and 2 Dots or **4 Craks** and **4 Bams** or 6 Dots and **6 Bams**, or **8 Craks** and 8 Dots, etc.—any Pungs of two suits with Even numbers.

Line 5: FF DDDD DDDD DDDD

Three colors, so you'll use all three Dragons: Red, White and Green.

369

This section only uses the numbers 3, 6 and 9. Only line 3 allows you some freedom.

Line 1: 3333 66 9999 DDDD (Any 1 Suit)

One color means one suit, including the Dragons.

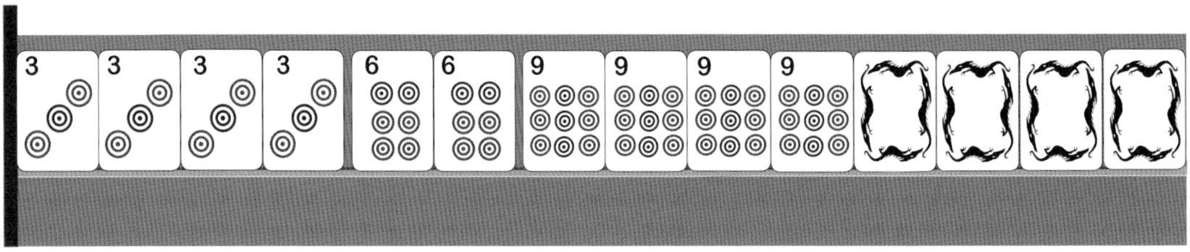

Soaps go with Dots

Line 2: FF 3333 6666 9999 or FF 3333 6666 9999 (1 or 3 Suits)

You can make this in one suit or all three.

Line 3: 33 66 99 3333 3333 (3 Suits; Kongs 3s, 6s, or 9s)

You see three colors, so three suits. You choose the suit for your Pairs. The Kongs must use the other two suits. You decide if you want them to be 3s, 6s, or 9s.

DO THIS

Take Pairs of **3 Bams**, **6 Bams**, and **9 Bams**. Use Kongs of 3 Dots and **3 Craks**. Do it with another combination, maybe using Kongs of 6s or 9s.

33 66 99 3333 3333 (3 Suits; Kongs 3s, 6s, or 9s)

At this point you're ready to tackle some of the harder parts of the Card: **2 4 6 8**; **Addition: Heavenly 11s**; the year area (here **The 21st Century**); and **Singles and Pairs.**

2 4 6 8

This section is also referred to as the "Evens." Unless you're told otherwise, you must copy what it says. Use the numbers you see and match them to your tiles. You have freedom only with the suits you use, but not in the way the suits are grouped within the hands.

Line 1: 22 44 DDDD 666 888 (Any 2 Suits and Non-Matching Dragons)

There are three colors, thus three suits. The Dragons are a different color from the numbers, so they're from the third suit, not represented by the numbers. If you're using Dots for the 2s and 4s, and Green Dragons in the middle, you must use Craks for your 6s and 8s. You saw this before: unmatched Dragons in the third line of the Consecutive Run. Here it's the same: one suit for the Pairs of 2s and 4s, another for the Pungs of 6s and 8s. The third suit will be your Dragons.

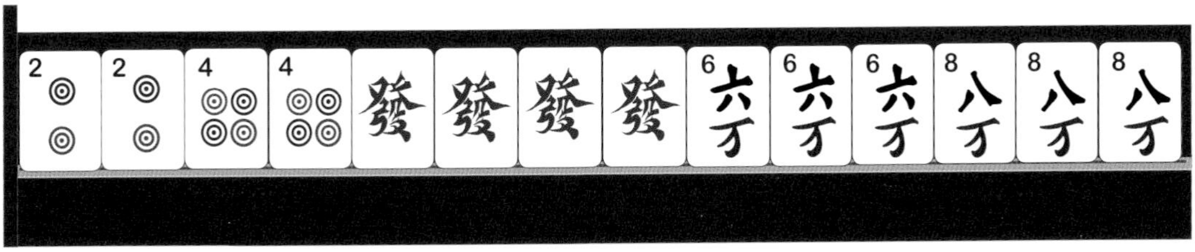

Dots and Craks with Green Dragons

DO THIS

Make the hand using Bams for your lower numbers, and Craks for the higher ones. Your Dragons will be Soaps.

Line 3: 22 44 444 666 8888 (3 Suits)

This hand has a **switchback**, two sets of the same numbers in different suits. (Until you "get it," switchbacks are hard to play.) You'll notice you have 4s in two suits, the first set corresponding with the Pair of 2s, and the second set the same as the Pungs of 6s. The Kong of 8s are the third suit.

DO THIS

Make the hand using Pairs of 2 and **4 Bams**, Pungs of 4 and 6 Dots, and a Kong of **8 Craks**. Try it again using other combinations. Get used to the idea of working with the same number, the 4s, in two different suits.

Line 5: 222 888 DDDD DDDD (3 Suits)

Once again, the hand requires three suits: the Pungs are one suit and the Dragons are the others.

Addition: Heavenly 11s

There's always a section with hands like this, often called Addition Hands. What does this mean? Only that the numbers add up to something. Here the different numbers total 11: 5 + 6 = 11; 4 + 7 = 11; 3 + 8 = 11. Once again you'll notice you have a choice: you can do it in one suit or three. You choose the numbers to combine. What you <u>must</u> have is a Pair of matching 1s. From there you can use the same suit for the other numbers, or two different suits.

Line 2: FFFF 4444 + 7777 = 11 or FFFF 4444 + 7777 = 11 (1 or 3 suits)

You'll notice you have a choice: one suit or three. You <u>must</u> have a Pair of 1s, but Jokers can be used elsewhere.

DO THIS

Pick whichever suits you want, using all three. Use two Jokers (but not for the 1s). Now do it using only one suit.

FFFF 4444 + 7777 = 11 (3 suits)

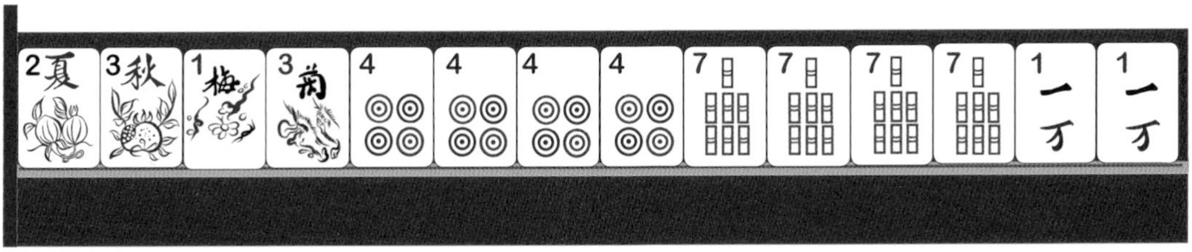

Heavenly 11s with three suits

21ST CENTURY

There's always a section involving the year. Our Card is more generic, so we feature years from our entire century, but it's the same concept as the year hands on the Card. What's most important here is for you to be able to wrap your head around the concept of the White Dragon, Soap, no matter what it looks like, being used as a "0" (Zero). The tile might look a bit like a squared off "0" (aka a frame), a bar of soap (no image), dragons chasing each other's tails, have a **B** or a **P**, or even be a Chinese symbol. No matter—in this section they are "0"s and only"0"s, and neutral. Caveat: a Soap is only a Zero when used for the year—it can never be used in a Consecutive Run.

Line 1: 222 1111 222 1111 (Any 2 Suits)

This one is very straightforward: Pungs of 2s and Kongs of 1s, two different suits, with matching 2s and 1s.

Line 2: NNNN E W SSSS 22 11 (These Nos. Only, Same Suit)

You must have an E and W, and your Pairs of 2s and 1s have to be the same suit as each other.

Line 3: FF 2222 1111 0000 (Any 2 Suits)

The parentheses here are a bit misleading, but this can happen. You need two different suits for the 1s and 2s. The Soaps are neutral because they're "0"s. They might be the same suit as the 1s or 2s, or not. It's up to you. You can make this hand with Kongs of Craks and Bams, Bams and Dots, or Dots and Craks. Even though the White Dragon is associated with the Dots, in these hands that doesn't matter. White Dragons here are purely and simply "0"s.

DO THIS

Make the hand with a Pair of Flowers, and Kongs of **2 Bams** and **1 Craks** and Soaps (the Zeros).

FF 2222 1111 0000

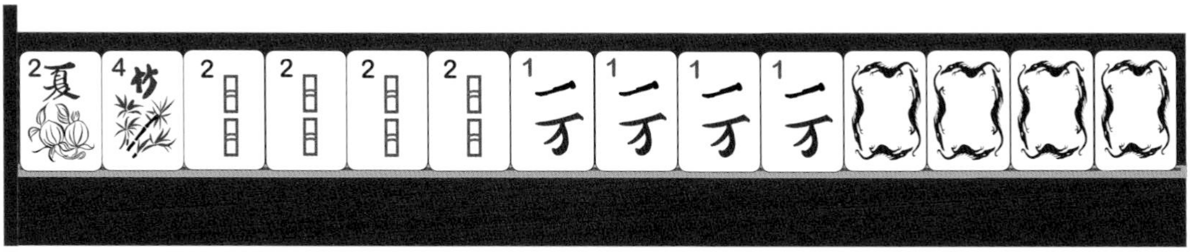

21st Century with Bams and Craks

Now make it with a Pair of Flowers, and Kongs of 2 Dots, **1 Craks**, and Soaps. Remember: Soaps are neutral. And use two Jokers where you can.

SINGLES AND PAIRS

Our last category is considered the most difficult on the card. This category has been called No Joker Hands, and you know why.

Line 1: NN EE WW SS 11 11 22 (3 Suits, These Nos. Only)

This is pretty clear. These numbers and Winds are the only ones you can use.

DO THIS

Make this hand using the two different suit Pairs of 1s and the third suit for the 2s.

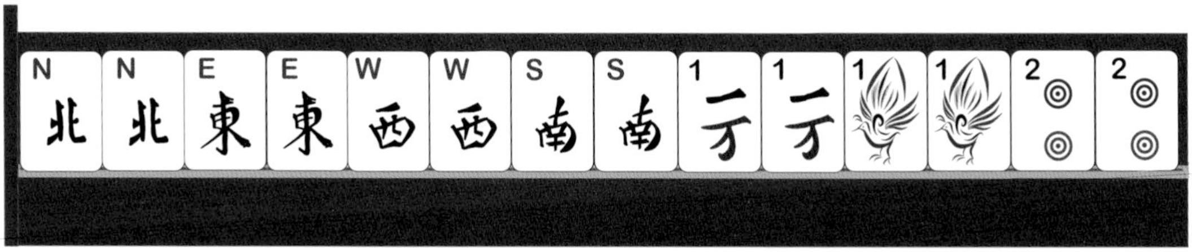

NEWS with 1s and 2s

Line 2: FF 11 22 33 44 55 DD (Any 1 Suit, 5 Consecutive Nos.)

One color means one suit with matching Dragons. You're free to pick the suit and where your run starts.

Line 3: FF 22 44 66 88 22 88 (Any 2 Suits, Last Pairs Only 2s and 8s)

Most of your Pairs will be in one suit, but the last 2s and 8s must be in another suit.

Line 7: FF 2019 2020 2021 (Any 3 Consecutive Years in the 21st Century, 3 Suits)

This type of hand is known each year as "**the Big Hand**." It's always about the year. As you can see, you need to have 2s in all three suits, but you choose your number run and you must have three Soaps. Nothing else works as a single "0": not Jokers, Green Dragons, Red Dragons, nothing.

DO THIS

Now make another run with different numbers and suits. Caveat: if you choose to have a run using 2022, all the 2s are treated as singles and pairs. Yes, there are a total of three 2s, but because they are arranged within the group as a single and a pair, no Jokers are allowed.

FF 2021 in Bams, 2022 in Dots, 2023 in Craks

Point Values

Let's talk about the numbers on the far right: the **Point Values**. These numbers represent the points, or cents, awarded to winners of each hand. (This can change depending on how the hand was won; see Chapter 7.) Given that there are so many 25-cent hands, we often talk about playing for quarters. If a hand has a 25 on the far right, it's considered easy. Some numbers are higher, indicating a more difficult hand. Do you see how high the value is in Singles and Pairs? That's because of the level of skill (and luck) it takes to make these hands. And "the Big Hand" gets the most points. Seasoned players will often go for the higher-point hands just for the fun and challenge.

Exposed and Concealed Hands

You'll learn about **discards**, **calling** for tiles, **exposures**, and when you can call in Chapter 7, but right now it's time to explain the **X**s and the **C**s on the far right of every hand. **X** indicates Exposed, meaning that if a tile is **discarded** by another player and you want it to complete a group of your tiles, you may **call** it. Then you must expose the entire **grouping** on top of your rack. **X** hands are the easiest to complete because you're able to call for discards. (Caveat: you can't call for a Single or a Pair other than for Mah Jongg, even if they're part of an **X** hand.) If the hand you're playing has a "**C**" at the far right, your hand's Concealed. Can't Call. If a tile you want is discarded, and it would complete the group you need, but it's not your Mah Jongg tile, you can't call it. This is a "Sad Mah Jongg Moment." A Concealed hand is considered a higher level of difficulty and it has a greater point value. Don't make the mistake of playing a Concealed hand as if it's Exposed and calling for a tile. You won't be able to play the hand you want, and you may be called **dead**. To avoid this, many players take a marker and highlight or underline concealed hands. But remember: as just stated, you can always call for the last tile you need for Mah Jongg even in a Concealed hand.

G&T Time:

Toby: One day I was playing with a group I didn't know. I called Mah Jongg! The woman across from me called my hand "dead." I said it was viable and pointed to it on the Card. She gasped, saying she hadn't seen that hand before. Well, it was March—12 months after the new Card came out!! If you don't know your Card in March, you never studied it. Read the back of the NMJL Card as well. It is the best cheat sheet, holding all kinds of information.

Gregg: One of the best things you can do is study the Card when it comes out. There are always confusing aspects, but there are online resources, and our website will help. Some hands are hard: make them over and over until you can wrap your head around them. This really helps.

Summary

- The National Mah Jongg League issues a new Card every April. The rules, tiles, categories and game usually remain the same, but the hands change.
- There are three colors on the Card. The colors don't represent a suit, but rather the suit must change when the color changes. One color indicates that you'll only use any one suit. Two colors mean any two suits, and three colors mean you must use all three.
- Usually the Card is divided into ten categories: the Year (or Century on ours), 2468 or Evens, Like Numbers, a Mystery Category (often Addition, changing each year), Quints, Consecutive Run, 13579 or Odds, Winds and Dragons, 369, and lastly, Singles and Pairs. Our Card reflects these sections.
- There are four types of tiles that do not have suits; Jokers, Zeros (Soaps are used when the number "0" is called for), Flowers and Winds (NEWS). Xs and Cs (for Exposed and Concealed) reflect what kind of hand it is: X means a player may call a discard to complete a grouping, but C only allows for a call when that tile is needed to complete Mah Jongg.
- Although no one tile is worth any more than any other tile, one hand might garner more points than another. The bold numbers to the right of each hand indicate how easy or difficult a hand is, and/or the amount of money one might win or lose.
- The Singles and Pairs section is the greatest challenge of all. The points to be gained are the highest on the Card.

Quiz

1. Does the color green on the Card mean you must use Bams only?
2. Can you use Jokers for Zeros?
3. Can you use all 7s instead of 1s in the section Like Numbers?
4. What is the least number of Jokers you need to make the second line down in Quints?
5. Can you call for a tile you need if there is a **C** at the end of the line?
6. Can you substitute any Wind for NEWS?
7. How many colors are on the Card?
8. How many Jokers can you use in the group NEWS or 2020?
9. What does an **X** mean at the end of a line?
10. How many Jokers can you use in the third line of the Singles and Pairs section?

Answers

1. No. The color on the Card doesn't indicate a specific suit. The number of colors in the hand just tells you how many suits you need to use.
2. Yes, just like any other group, as long as there are three or more identical tiles in a row in the group.
3. Yes. You can use any number you like, between 1 and 9. They just have to all be the same numbers.
4. Two Jokers are needed for this hand.
5. You can only call a tile for Mah Jongg.
6. No. When NEWS is written, you must have those tiles.
7. There are three colors, each representing a suit, but not a specific one.
8. You can't use any Jokers in NEWS or in any year. These are considered singles and pairs.
9. **X** means you may call a discard to expose the group of three or more identical tiles that match the grouping you need on the Card. You're able to use a Joker to complete the group if you don't have all the tiles you need.
10. None. You can never use a Joker for a single or a pair.

2 SUM
3 AUT
VALUES
WINDS - DRAGONS
11111 22 33 44444
FF 2222 8888 DDDD
FF 2222 4444 6666 88
2222 4444 6666 8888
LIKE NUMBERS
LUCKY "13"
2468

Chapter 5

Organizing Tiles and Picking Directions for Your Hand

After the deal, each player will have 13 tiles, except for East, who'll have 14, and a bit of an advantage. It's now time to see what tiles you have, and arrange them. You have to figure out some areas of the Card (or here, our Card) that might work with the tiles you have. We'll help by giving you an overview on how to organize your tiles to figure out your strengths, and then we'll take it from there. We're going to show you how we organize our tiles.

Once the deal is over, turn over your tiles and put them on the angled side of the rack. Place any Jokers you're lucky enough to get on the far left, with your Flowers next to them. Arrange tiles by suit and numerical order to see what area is strongest, if you have **Pairs** or **Multiples** (three or more), and what tiles are related to others you have. Are most of your tiles in one suit, lower than 5 or higher, closely grouped in number, Odds, Evens? You get it. Put your Winds and Dragons on the far right.

As you know, certain groups go together. The White Dragons, when they're Dragons and not Zeros, are always associated with the Dots, the Red Dragons with the Craks, and the Green with Bams. Typically Winds, Dragons and Flowers go together, and often North and Souths go with Odd numbers, and East and West (think E for East and Evens) go with the Evens.

The goal in organizing tiles is to try to find a pattern that's strong enough to choose a category (section, area) or a specific hand to pursue. Jokers and Flowers go with most of the hands on the card, so we'll place them near each other.

You need to find a couple of areas where you think you have some strengths. Find four or more tiles that might be related to each other. Really look and think. A Joker can stand in for tiles you're missing. You need to figure out which tiles might help you.

Decisions, decisions

G&T Time:

Gregg: I know it sounds silly, but many players talk about "listening" to the tiles. Of course we hear them when they touch each other or the rack, and when they're discarded, but we mean something else here. It often seems that the tiles are trying to "tell" us what direction to go in. Best to be a good listener from the beginning.

Toby: I get really happy when the tiles are very clear—but since they have been known to mumble, I have to be really attentive.

At this point your tiles should be talking to you, and it is always important to pay attention. We think it best to really look at each tile on your rack and say its name in your head. (You're starting to listen to the tiles!) We find it much easier to get an idea of patterns this way, rather than just doing a quick look and reacting as if we have really given them all a chance to tell their story, while we've missed the ending....

Figure out a few areas where you have strengths. Start with Flowers if you have them. They open up a lot of hands. Look for Pairs and Multiples, and see if you can use all of them in one hand. You are searching for the best use of your tiles, and this is a good start.

> Sometimes you may have a pair that does not work with the rest of your tiles. Suppose you have mostly Winds and Dragons and a pair of 2 Bams. Don't be fooled by something that seemingly looks good. Ask yourself "Will it help my hand?" If not, forget about it.

It is usually best not to build a hand requiring pairs if you don't have at least half of the pair you need. Remember: Jokers need a crowd, so even if you have lots of Jokers, they can't be part of a pair. Look for hands that don't need a pair if you don't have them from the beginning.

Do you have any strong suits? Are the numbers odds, evens, 3s 6s and 9s, or numbers close to each other? These will help you figure out your hand. If your tiles are related in some way, you're off to a grand start! Remember: Dragons are often grouped with numbers and Winds, and if you've got those, you have even more strength. You can find those areas pretty easily on the card. Do you have a pair of 1s? Maybe Heavenly 11s is for you. The Consecutive Number area gives you the most freedom, and it's pretty easy. If we have a lot of numbers close to each other, we do what we call the "Number Clumper." We keep tiles within three or four numbers of each other. See how many close numbers you have.

> In some areas of the Card (as on the NMJL Card), your negative can actually be a positive! This is the case with the first hand of **2468.** You'll see that the first line has Pairs in one suit and Pungs in another suit. If you have Dragons that aren't associated with those suits, they help you here. But in **Like Numbers,** second line down: matching Dragons are what you want. So you'll have to do some important thinking from the beginning about who goes out with whom, and when!!

Now that you've a broad understanding, we'll take this step by step to see how to arrange tiles to figure out what they're saying (i.e., how they're guiding your choices).

Tiles to Work With

Remember: colors only represent suits, not *which* suit. We're sure it's easier for you to analyze your hand if you see Crak written in red, and Bam in green, but you know a color is just a suit, not a specific suit.

For purposes of this chapter, when we're working with the tiles, we'll be abbreviating them as follows: Bams will be B, so if you have a 1 Bam it will read **1B**. Craks are **C**. If there's a number with a D, it's a Dot, so a 1 Dot will be a 1D. Be careful, because this can be confusing: Dragons are Ds, but they will not have a number in front of them. If it has a number, it is a Dot. If *any* Dragon is allowed, Dragon will be a D, but if there are specific ones called for, a Red Dragon will be **R**, Green will be G, and White will be Wh (although this does not appear on the Card). F is a Flower and J a Joker. But remember: the colors on our Card (or the Card) do NOT indicate which suits. We're doing it this way here because, for a beginner, it's clearer.

DO THIS
Take out our Card. Deal yourself these tiles and arrange them in this way. Lucky you, you're East and you're starting off with 14 tiles.

2D 5C 4D 8B 9C 1B 3C E S R J F 8C 8C

Jokers and Flowers

Certainly when we look at our tiles and see a Joker, our hearts start to beat a bit faster. We have freedom. As we've said, place your Jokers on the far left and keep them out of the mix. They can be helpful in lots of groups, so don't forget about them. Flowers make a lot of hands possible, so put them on the left, too—in the order in which they usually appear on the Card—after the Jokers. Remember: all Flowers are equal.

DO THIS
Move the Joker to the left, followed by the Flower:

J F 2D 5C 4D 8B 9C 1B 3C E S R 8C 8C

Suits

It's time to arrange your tiles in suits, by number. Doing this will help you see which suit has the most tiles. Although some people organize by numbers, we think it best to start organizing by suits.

DO THIS
Place each of your suits together in a consecutive run. For instance, place a 2 Dot and a 4 Dot in that order. Then place your Craks in order: **3 Crak, 5 Crak, 8 Crak, 8 Crak, 9 Crak**. And then your Bams: **1 Bam, 8 Bam**. It doesn't matter which suit goes first, second or third. We like to place our suit with the most tiles after the Flowers. Your hand now looks like this:

J F 3C 5C 8C 8C 9C 2D 4D 1B 8B E S R

Your strongest suit is <u>Craks</u>.

Numbers

Let's see what kind of numbers you have. Put the tiles in numerical order so that you can see same numbers, Evens, and Odds.

DO THIS

J F 1B 2D 3C 4D 5C 8C 8C 8B 9C E S R

Half of your numbers are in the higher range on the card, 5–9, and you don't have Evens that would go together. You only have two numbers that fit into **3 6 9**, so that's not strong either. But you do have three 8s, so that's a good start. You have five numbers 5 and above, with a few consecutive ones, and a pair.

Winds and Dragons

Put these tiles on the far right to start, with the tiles by suit.

DO THIS

Group your Winds together going North, East, West, South (NEWS), the way you see it on the Card:

J F 3C 5C 8C 8C 9C 2D 4D 1B 8B E S R

There's really nothing to work with just looking at the Winds. Let's see if you have a good amount of Winds and Dragons.

DO THIS

Put all your Dragons, Winds and Flowers together—our Card has them as a grouping:

J 3C 5C 8C 8C 9C 2D 4D 1B 8B E S R F

There's still little to get excited about. But let's try the Dragons with the suits they go with.

DO THIS

Put your Dragon with the matching suits.

J F 3C 5C 8C 8C 9C R 2D 4D 1B 8B E S

Grouping your tiles this way, you'll notice you have the Dragon that goes with the Craks, giving you possible strength in that area.

Time to Assess

So let's try looking at some deals by section of our Card. Let's look at each category to see where your strengths are.

21st Century

You have no White Dragons or 1s so forget that area.

2468

You have five evens: 2 Dot, 4 Dot, **8 Crak**, **8 Crak,** 8 Bam, but they're not part of the way the numbers and Dragons are arranged on the card. So not this area.

Like Numbers

You have three 8s, a Flower, a Joker and a Red Dragon that could go with the **8 Craks**. This could work.

Addition: Heavenly 11s

You have no 1 Pairs, so forget this.

Quints

You don't have enough Jokers or the right combination of Dragons, Winds and numbers, so move on.

Consecutive Run

Look at the **8 Craks**, and the **9 Crak**. You have a good start with the **Craks**, Flower and matching Dragon.

1 3 5 7 9

You don't have enough odds in the right categories: Low, High or Run. No for now.

Winds and Dragons

You have two unrelated Winds, and one Dragon. Keep moving.

3 6 9

You have one **3 Bam** and one **9 Crak**. This is really weak.

Singles and Pairs

You don't have enough pairs, and you have a Joker. This is not the right place.

Where do you go? You're strongest in the **Like Number** and **Consecutive Run** areas of the card. This is what you'll think about.

Let's try another group of tiles.

DO THIS

Select the following tiles and put them in front of you. Organize them this way:

J J F 4D 7D 8D 9D 1B 7B 4C R R E

Of course you are thrilled you have 2 Jokers and 1 Flower to start with. So work your way through the Card to see if you can find an area that's a starting point. The first section, **21st Century**, does not work at all. For **2 4 6 8** you only have three even numbers, two 4s of different suits, so this doesn't look strong. For **Like Numbers** you have two 4s, so that might work. Plus you have a Flower and two Jokers, so a possible five tiles. And if you could get another **4 Crak**, you could use the two related **Red** Dragons, meaning a possible six tiles for this area, so think about this one. In **Heavenly 11s** you don't have any 1 Pairs so probably not, but you have three suits with one **1 Bam**, the **4 Crak** and the 7 Dot, plus you have a Flower and two Jokers, so don't give up on this yet.

You have a possible six tiles, but you're nowhere if you don't get another **1 Bam**. This area is weak. **Quint:** You don't have enough of anything and better to use those Jokers somewhere else. **Consecutive Run**: You have a Flower, and a nice run of Dots: 7 Dot, 8 Dot, 9 Dot. Your best bet for using these tiles is the third hand down. Notice you need Flowers (you have one), two consecutive numbers (you have a **7 Bam** and an 8 Dot), and nonmatching Dragons (the two **Red** ones!) For this hand you have seven tiles, not a bad number to start with. **1 3 5 7 9** is very weak, as is **Winds and Dragons.** For **3 6 9** you only have one number. And don't even think about **Singles and Pairs**—you have two Jokers that could never be used in that section.

So what does this mean for you? Give up on the **Heavenly 11s** and concentrate on the **Like Numbers** and **Consecutive Numbers**.

DO THIS

Deal yourself 14 tiles (You can be East.) Arrange them and figure out what your strengths are, what numbers you have the most of, or areas on our Card that can possibly work. Keep dealing yourself new tiles until you feel somewhat comfortable with the sections and the decision process.

Congratulations! You understand how to figure out a direction for your hand. From now on, try to keep the tiles you like on the left part of your rack, and the tiles you don't like on the right side. This will be helpful in the next phase of the game, and hopefully will prevent you from mistakenly getting rid of a tile you really want.

Summary

Organizing your tiles is often a matter of your own personal style. Here is simply what we do after the deal: we place our Jokers on the far left and our Flowers to the right of the Jokers. But as a player, you need to move tiles around when you first get them, trying different fits. Organize each suit in consecutive runs. Keep your Winds together in the order they appear on the card: N E W S. Place Dragons with the Winds, and then with the suit they are "married" to. Try organizing the tiles in numerical order to see if you have a lot of numbers close together. Look at every tile you have and try to figure out if there is a way you can work with it. You may think you are starting out doing the 2 4 6 8 second line down because you have a lot of 8s, but you suddenly find you have Flowers and some matching Dragons—now it may be time to go for the **Like Numbers**. The key is to be mentally flexible, and to notice new possibilities.

G&T Time:

Gregg: I have to organize by suit. I put the tiles together, in ascending order. Only then do I count: how many Odds, Evens, Winds and Dragons? Do I have 3, 6, 9 as a possible group? Then I move them to numerical order. (I love that "Number Clumper" thing.) I find really looking at the tiles and saying their names in my head helps me to see what I have.

Toby: My mother had her tiles inside out and backwards! Just kidding, but I would circle the table and be completely baffled by my mom's lack of organization. Well, let me tell you, she was a shark! She simply had her own style that absolutely worked for her. I like to look at my tiles and see what section is calling out to me. I don't exactly choose a hand in the beginning but rather collect and collect until a specific hand is obvious. Let the tiles lead you.

Quiz

1 What are the rules about organizing your tiles?

2 Do you incorporate your Jokers into a possible hand after you have been dealt your tiles?

3 In what order do you place your Winds on your rack?

4 Why would you position your Flowers on the far left?

5 Why would you keep your Dragons with the suit they go with?

Answers

1 There are none. There are guidelines.

2 No. Keep them separate until they can only fill a specific need.

3 **NEWS**

4 That's where they are usually found on the card.

5 Typically, that is how you find them on the card.

Exercise

Take out the following tiles and see what you would do. Answers for our Card follow. The website will show you sections for the current NMJL Card.

What areas would you think about:

1 **F 1D 2D 6D 2B 3B 5B 7B 4C 7C 9C N E**

2 **J F F 1D 3D 3D 4D 6D 1B 8B 9B 7C 9C**

3 **J F 3D 5D 7D 2C 3C 6C 6C 7C 9C 7B Wh**

4 **F 5D 7D 8D 8D 7C 9C 1B 9B N E G R**

5 **J 1B 3C 5C 8C 8C 9C 6D 6D W W W N**

6 **1C 2C 7C 1D 2D 4D 3B 4B G G G R W**

7 **F 2B 2B 5B 5B 8B 2 D 4D 6D 9D 3C 8C G**

8 **7C 7C 8C 9C 4B 5B 7B 4D E W W G Wh**

9 **J F F 1D 9D 1B 8B 6C S S E G R**

10 **2C 4C 5C 7C 9C 9C 1B 3B 4B 5B 4D E W**

Answers for our Card

1 Using Number Clumping, you have six tiles between 1 and 5. Keep all those and hope for either something in **Consecutive Numbers** or **Like Numbers.**

2 Think about **3 6 9**, or **Like Numbers** with **1s**, **3s** or **9s**.

3 Think about **3 6 9**, **Like Numbers** with **3s** and **7s**, and **Consecutive Run** using mixed suits: the **F**, **6Cs**, 7B and **Wh**.

4 Think about **Consecutive Run**. No need for 1B, **N** or **E**. The Dragons might work with these.

5 Maybe a **Quint** using the Ws and one of your pairs, but you need Flowers. **3 6 9** is possible. You don't need the 1B, **5C** or **N**.

6 Number Clumping: Try the **Consecutive Run** with low numbers between 1 and 3: 1C 2C **1D 2D** 3B or **Consecutive Run** with **1C 2C** 3B 4B, but hold onto your Dragons—you might be able to use them.

7 **2 4 6 8** is the best bet. Even though you have a pair of 5 Bams, you can't use them.

8 You could hope for **1 3 5 7 9** Upper Odds, using 5 Bam and 7 Bam with **7 Crak** and **9 Crak**, and **Wh** (line 6). You don't need the 4s or Winds. Maybe the Dragons for possible **Like Numbers** with **7s**.

9 Think about **1 3 5 7 9** 5th line down using **Fs**, **J**, 1 Bam, **9 Dot**, **R** or **Winds** and **Dragons #2**.

10 Try **1 3 5 7 9** either Line 4 or 7.

E
東
6
六萬
S

Part 2

Playing the Game

Chapter 6

The Charleston

"The Charleston," with apologies to John Held, Jr.

The Charleston brings to mind the Roaring '20s and that beautiful town in South Carolina. Who knew it could have something to do with mahjong? Those ladies at the NMJL did, back in the '30s. It's a series of tile **passes**, named after the dance craze in the 1920s that took the United States by storm, as did mahjong. The moves, similar to the "back forward, forward back" of the dance, have a rightful place on the game table. Who says we don't dance on tables any more? We do the Charleston!

The NMJL looked upon this phase of the game as a chance for players to improve their hands, right after the tiles are dealt, ridding themselves of unwanted tiles, while hoping to get better ones. Remember we mentioned keeping the tiles you like for your hand on the left side of the rack, and the ones you don't need on the right? You're about to find out why.

Right after the deal, three of you have 13 tiles, <u>but</u> East has 14. After the tiles have been organized on the hidden side of the racks (Chapter 5), players do a series of passes—usually seven. These exchanges are key to shaping your hand. You must keep <u>two</u> things (at a minimum) in your head during this part of the game: you want to build the best hand possible for yourself, and you don't want to be helpful to others. You'll understand this better later in the chapter.

As soon as you've organized your tiles you'll have to decide what to keep and what to pass. You'll give and get three tiles each time. Look at the tiles you receive, and see if they can possibly help. Sometimes one tile can open up your eyes to a whole new possibility, even a Section of the card. Keep what's helpful and pass what's not. Sometimes you'll realize you can do something with that tile you just passed—don't worry, it just may come back to you! So plan for that if you can.

Right now we'll go over the pass sequences. Of course there are quirks to this ritual. We'll discuss how to make the most of this phase a bit later.

ROLLOR

The Charleston is a set sequence that's hard to remember. Someone came up with an acronym: ROLLOR. The first round is R=Right O=Over (aka Opposite) L=Left, and second is L=Left O=Over R=Right.

It begins when each player has selected three tiles to pass to the player on the **R**ight (R). Keeping your tiles low so that others can't see them, place them in the corner of the table, face down. As soon as you've passed your tiles, you can pick up the three tiles passed to you on your left. Figure out if the new arrivals help your hand. If they don't, get rid of them in another pass. The same is true of all tiles you receive during the Charleston.

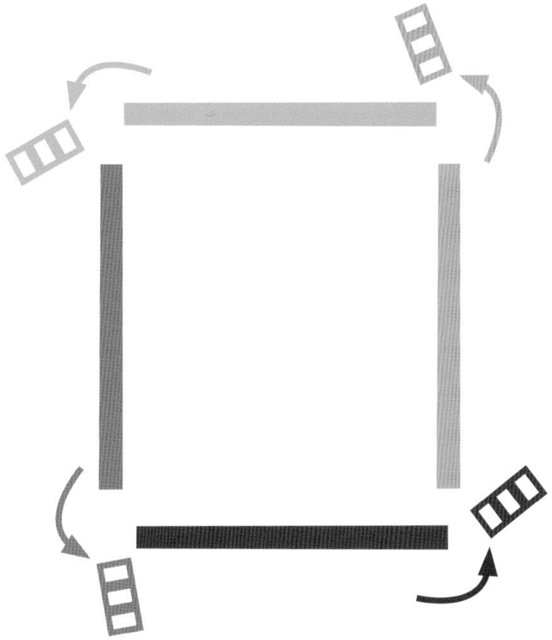

First pass: to the Right.

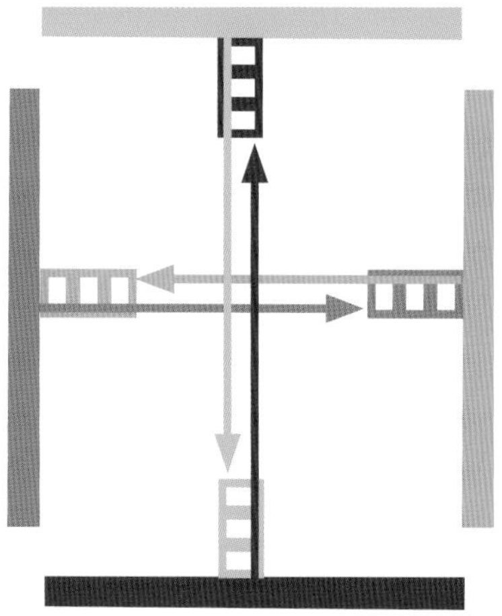

Second pass goes to Opposite player.

Once everyone has <u>completed</u> the first pass, it's time for **O**ver (O). Place three unwanted tiles face down in front of the player across from you. They in turn, will place three unwanted tiles face down in front of you. The easiest visual cue is to have your three tiles lined up in a perpendicular manner to the opposite player's rack. Remember to pass your tiles so that nobody can see them.

Third pass: it's the first Left.

Once everyone has taken the passes, the next one is First **L**eft (L). Place three tiles facedown in your left corner. Again, you can pick up the tiles passed to you on your right as soon as you've passed yours. Interesting things can happen here at the first Left pass, but you'll have to read to the end of the chapter to find out what they are!

G&T Time:

Gregg: We like to have fun with all parts of the game when we're not in a serious competition, naming our passes. I call my First Left the little Ranch House (tiles passed flat) and the Second the little Colonial (tiles stacked).
Toby: With a nod to fashion, the First Left can be a beret (passed flat) and the Second a chapeau or top hat.

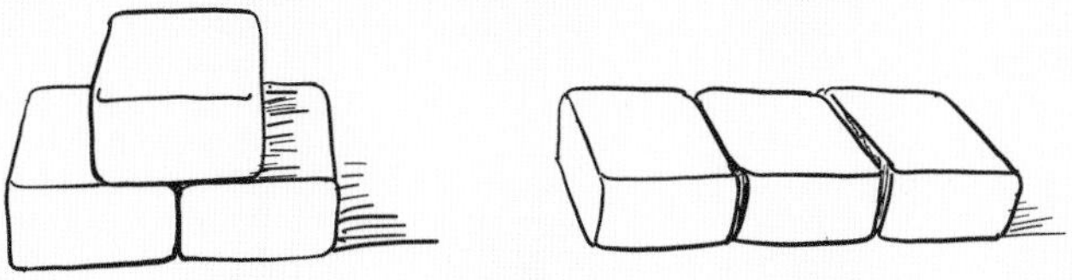

Colonial and ranch, aka "chapeau and beret"

Now it's time for the Second **L**eft (L). We need a visual cue to indicate this. Tiles are two-tiered: two on the bottom and one on top, telling everyone "second left." This is the <u>only</u> time in all of Mah Jongg that you will pass tiles in a "tower."

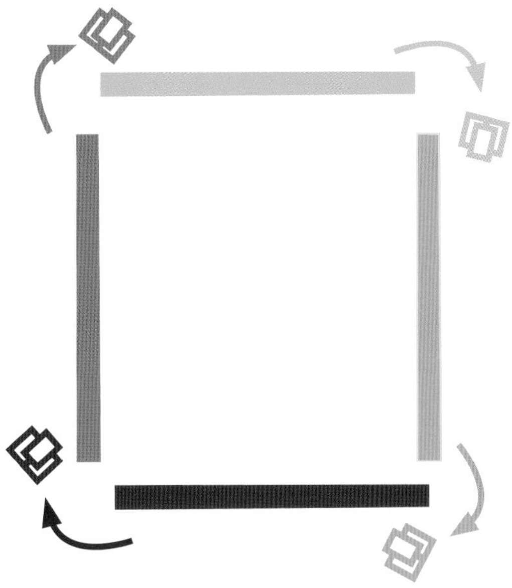

Fourth pass: it's the second Left, two tiles on the bottom and one on top.

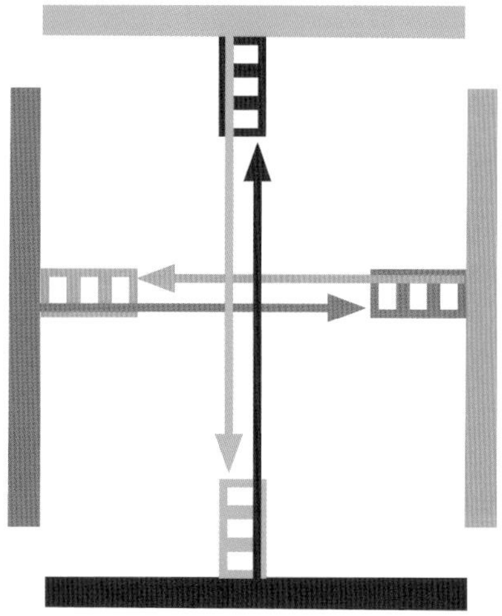

Fifth pass, to the Opposite player.

Now pass three tiles **O**ver (O). Again, be aware of the placement of your tiles. They should be in front of that player, perpendicular to the rack if possible.

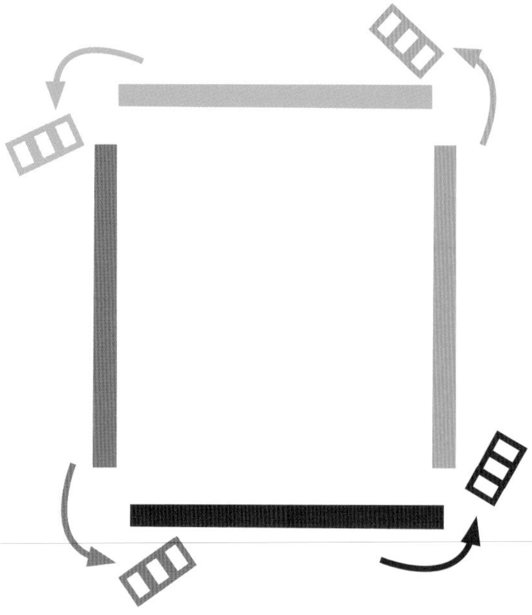

This is the final Right pass.

The next pass is the Final **R**ight (R): three tiles facedown in your right corner. But we bet you figured that one out!

We now do what's called an **Optional** Over, or **Courtesy** Pass. This pass is just what is says…optional. You choose to pass between zero and three tiles; the lowest number is what both of you will pass. Example: Two players are across from each other. One player wants to pass two tiles while the other player doesn't want to pass any. No tiles will be passed. The other two players are also ready to pass. One would like to pass three and the other player two.

They pass two tiles to each other. It doesn't matter who announces how many tiles they would like to pass first, whoever says the lowest number gets to have that amount passed between them. And believe it or not, quite often they both pass the exact same tiles. Some tiles are just not loved during certain games.

When you're doing the Charleston, and ready to receive the pass, make a gap in your rack where you will drop the tiles you've been passed. Close the gap when you have the pass, then reorganize. If you do this, other players won't know if they've helped you in any way. Evaluate your new arrivals: one tile can make you see your hand in a whole different light. Put your unwanted tiles on the right side of the rack, ready to be passed next.

Using the Charleston

The goal of the game is to complete a hand on the Card and call "Mah Jongg!" The Charleston is your first chance to move in this direction. As a beginner, seeing the tiles for the first time on your rack can seem daunting. As we discussed in Chapter 5, take a look at your 13 or 14 tiles. See if you have Jokers, Flowers, Pairs, Pungs, Odds or Evens, Dragons, Winds or several tiles in one suit. Any of these can lead you to a hand or a section. Let's say you've been dealt eight tiles in one suit: you might just go for a one-color or one-suit hand. Imagine the suit you are collecting is Bams. With every pass, you might collect more Bams. As your hand changes, maybe a specific section will become obvious to you. During the Charleston, you'll receive tiles, some new and some familiar, that can help you develop your hand.

Suppose you "think" you have nothing. Maybe you have three Wind tiles. You might just start collecting every Wind that comes your way and whoa! By the end of the passes, you could just be on the way to a winning hand of Winds. Pay attention to the tiles passed. Try to remember what's going around—for two different reasons. The first is if your hand is going nowhere but lots of something (often Winds) is going around (this happens all the time!), you can start collecting that. The second is that when you don't see a tile again, it means someone is using it. This can help you later in the game.

What if you're between two hands in two different sections? Yes, you have to make a decision, but often in Mah Jongg, the right one isn't obvious. Just do your best. You have seven tiles for one hand and nine tiles for another hand. It's not always about how many tiles you have. Do you have the pairs in one hand but not in the other hand—the one with more tiles? Is one hand concealed? These answers can change everything.

Once you've figured out an area of strength, you need to select three tiles you don't need—your "garbage." You will pass three unwanted tiles each time.

How to Pass Defensively

As we said earlier, you want to improve your own hand. But: here's where the "not helping anyone else" part comes in. Make your passes as "mushy" as possible. Try your best to pass three tiles that don't go together. Keep your Pairs, Pungs, and Kongs whenever possible. If you must pass those tiles, break them up into several passes. Avoid passing the same numbered tiles.

Try not to pass Flowers and Soaps. These passes could be helping another player, and that's not your job. You cannot pass a Joker. Why would anyone want to? They might be close to Mah Jongg and don't want to break up what they've got. For you, a bad pass is one that will help another player, and a good one is one that will help you! In Mah Jongg it's all about YOU!

Example:
Bad Passes

1 Bam **1 Dot 1 Crak**
North South South
2 Crak 3 Crak Red
Flower Flower Flower

Good Passes

6 Bam **Red 3 Dot**
North 9 Crak 2 Dot
4 Bam **7 Crak East**
1 Bam **8 Crak South**

Mushy!

Making Decisions

Let's be real: the Charleston is scary, at least to beginning players. But all of us so often feel we don't have a clear concept of what we want to do. That's normal. Work with your best tiles—there have to be at least four—and start from there. We'll go through some practice deals and choices.

DO THIS

Take out our Card. Deal yourself:

F F 3B 6B 9B 2D 8D 9D 3C 3C R N S

What to pass? It seems that you are pretty strong in your numbers 3, 6 and 9. You want to give a mushy pass, so maybe pass your 2 Dot, 8 Dot and one of your Winds. From now on, you'll keep every 3, 6 and 9 tile no matter which suit and see which hand speaks to you at the end of the passes. Take your rejects and pass them to the right.

DO THIS

Take these tiles:

J J F 2D 2D 6B 8B 9B 4C 7C 8C R S

The Evens seem strong. You can pass the odds and the South easily and still hold onto all evens. Start collecting them with every pass and see if a hand emerges for you in the **2 4 6 8** section. If you go in this direction, and you have a choice between giving away an even or an odd, give away the odd. As long as you have three tiles to pass, you should collect all tiles that fit into the category you're aiming for. Take the South, **9 Bam** and **7 Crak** and pass them.

DO THIS

Take these tiles:

J J F F 3C 3C 6C 9C 3D 5D 7B 8B E S

You're between two types of hands: **Like Numbers** and **3 6 9**. Pass the tiles that don't fit in with either scenario. Take the **5D**, **E**, **S** and pass them.

Let's say you have completed the first round of the Charleston. You find yourself with this scenario and you have to choose between two possible hands.

DO THIS

Take these tiles:

3B 3B 5B 5B 7B 9B 9B 1C 1C 5C 9C 9C N S

You have a very strong beginning here with all **Bams**, and it looks like a no-brainer to choose the first hand in **1 3 5 7 9: 11 333 5555 777 99**. You have seven tiles for this hand, but you're missing a pair of **1**s. But look a bit harder—notice the 2nd hand down in **1 3 5 7 9**. You can use your **1 Craks**, **3 Bams** and **5 Bams**, and you have six tiles. You don't have the **3 Craks** you need, but the actual game has not even started. You can always use Jokers for all of the tiles you do not have yet. Get rid of your North and South, and part with your **7 Bam**.

G&T Time:

Gregg: I tell all my students to try to keep two sections in their head, at least at the beginning of the passes. Don't narrow it down to one section, or even one hand, unless it is extremely strong.

Toby: I had a student, one of my friends, a very smart and capable businesswoman. As a beginner, she consistently went for five or more hands at once. She never won a game and dropped out. If you can keep your hand focused and simple, you'll have a better chance of winning.

Possible Missing Steps in the Charleston

A couple quirky (there's that word again!) things can happen during the Charleston: the **Blind Pass**, and **Stopping the Charleston**. We'll go over what each one is, and reasons why they may occur.

The Blind Pass

The **Blind Pass** is when you pass, sight unseen (thus blind) tiles that were passed to you. It's used when players don't have three unwanted tiles. There are only <u>two</u> times you can do a Blind Pass: the <u>First Left</u> and the <u>Final Right</u>. Only then are players allowed to pass <u>any</u> number of tiles, up to three, from those just given to them.

Here's how it works. Say one player, on the First Left or the Final Right, wants to do a blind pass because they only want to part with one or two tiles, or even none. (Some players refer to this as **Stealing**.)

On first left, purple player has three tiles to pass, but blue player has only two.

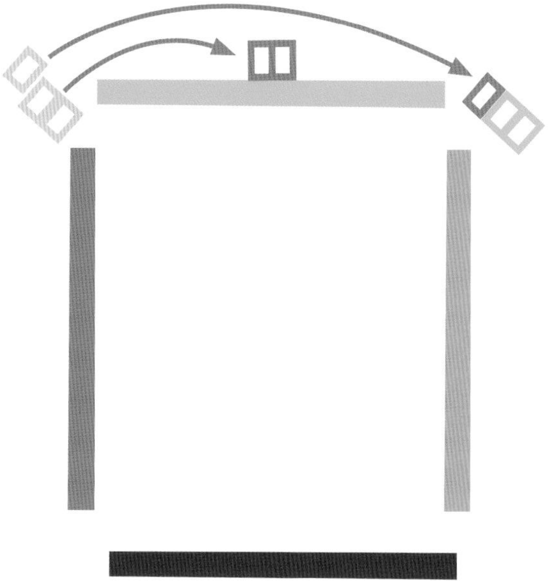

One tile is taken from Purple's pass and added to Blue's pass, allowing Blue to pass three tiles.

The player who only wants to part with two tiles takes one tile without looking (blind) from the pass they just got, and adds it to their two, thus passing three tiles. They're just adding two new tiles to their rack.

Think about it: they parted with two tiles, "borrowed one" to turn their two into three, and got two new tiles instead of the other players, who got three "new" tiles. If they want to pass one tile, they would take two others, sight unseen, from those tiles passed to them and move three along, thus adding one new tile to their rack. What if they don't want to pass any? That's fine too. They'd take all three tiles given and pass them along. But if a player looks at the tiles they get before a blind pass, that player is "**dead**" and no longer a part of the game. Remember: The Blind Pass can only happen on the First Left and the Final Right.

Stopping the Passes

There is only one time this can happen, and it's just after the First Left.

At this point, anyone can stop the passes. If you want to stop the Charleston, say so right away, while people are still arranging the tiles they got in the First Left. It's imperative that the player who'd like to stop the passes says so before others look at the Second Left. If anyone has seen that pass, it's too late. After the First Left, often players ask, "Do we want to do the next round?" This allows everyone to assess where they are.

Why would anyone want to stop? Most players avoid stopping the passes because they hope to acquire more tiles they need for a hand. But there are exceptional moments in Mah Jongg. Say you are going for a Singles and Pairs hand, and you're two tiles away after the first Charleston (**R**ight **O**ver **L**eft). Well, the last thing you want to do is pass part of a pair you need. Or suppose you're playing a hand and the only tile you need is to complete a pair. You stop. Sometimes you're between two hands; usually choose one and keep on going.

If the Charleston has been stopped, everyone still has the opportunity to do an Optional Pass.

Summary

- **The Charleston is a series of passes after the deal, with the goal of nearing a hand or a Section. We use the acronym R O L L O R to help us remember where to pass our tiles: "Right Over Left," "Left Over Right." Over means the person Opposite (across from) you. Anyone can stop the passes after the First Left, but the Optional one is still possible. You can do a blind pass on the first Left and the final Right. You "borrow" tiles, without looking, from the tiles you have just received so that you're passing a total of three tiles. No peeking. The Optional pass is the last across (Over), when all other passes have been completed. You both choose the number of tiles, from zero to three, that you'd like to exchange. The lowest number is what you'll both pass.**
- **Always stack the Second Left to visually scream, "We are on the Second Left."**
- **It is "illegal" to pass a Joker. Try not to pass Pairs, Pungs, Flowers and Soaps. When aiming for a particular category or section, keep everything in that group: pass what's not in the section. When choosing a hand, it isn't only about how many tiles you have but do you have or need pairs, is it a concealed hand, and do you have Jokers, Flowers? If you have to get rid of a pair, don't pass them both at the same time. Divide them up, passing one at a time.**

Quiz

1 How many passes are there?
2 When can you stop the passes?
3 What does ROLLOR mean?
4 What's a Blind pass?
5 What's a "good" pass?
6 What's a "bad" pass?
7 When do you "stack" tiles?
8 Which tile is "illegal" to pass?
9 Who determines how many tiles to pass on the Optional Over?
10 Name two reasons you might go for one hand over another even though the hand you're choosing has fewer tiles.

Answers

1 Seven, unless the Charleston is stopped. In that case there are three passes, and an optional Over.
2 You can stop after the First Left.
3 ROLLOR describes the direction you'll pass your tiles: Right Over (Opposite) Left, Left Over Right.
4 A Blind pass is when any player wants to pass fewer than three tiles on the first left or the last right, borrowing, sight unseen, the number of tiles needed to make up the required threesome.
5 A "good" pass has unrelated tiles.
6 A "bad" pass contains related tiles.
7 The Second Left is always stacked.
8 It's "illegal" to pass a Joker.
9 The person asking to pass the lowest number determines the amount.
10 You have the Pairs. The hand can be exposed, which is usually easier to win than a concealed hand.

Chapter 7

Overview of Play

Some of us call the entry into the world of Mah Jongg one of the best parts of our lives. The game can save us in times of trouble, and cause laughter to boost our spirits. Sometimes our hoped-for hand does not come together, and we're sad…until the next game begins. When we sit around the table, socializing with others, and worrying about which hand to make and where the tile we need might be hiding, all we're thinking about is the game. This is one of the big appeals of Mah Jongg: we focus on the tiles and forget all the other things we're worried about in our lives. Mah Jongg is a real escape when you sit down to play.

Place the top half-inch of your NMJL Card under your rack, ending right where the actual hands begin. Align the bottom of your card with the edge of the table. This leaves the most amount of real estate in the middle of the table for dealing.

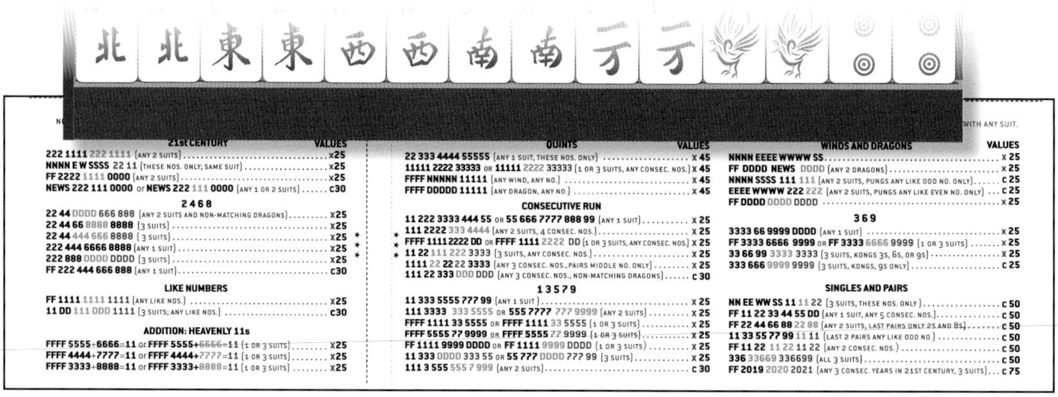

WITH ANY SUIT.

21st CENTURY — VALUES
222 1111 222 1111 (ANY 2 SUITS) x25
NNNN E W SSSS 22 11 (THESE NOS. ONLY; SAME SUIT) x25
FF 2222 1111 0000 (ANY 2 SUITS) x25
NEWS 222 111 0000 or NEWS 222 111 0000 (ANY 1 OR 2 SUITS) c30

2 4 6 8
22 44 DDDD 666 888 (ANY 2 SUITS AND NON-MATCHING DRAGONS) x25
22 44 66 8888 8888 (3 SUITS) x25
22 44 444 666 8888 (3 SUITS) .... x25 *
222 444 6666 8888 (ANY 1 SUIT) .... x25 *
222 888 DDDD DDDD (3 SUITS) .... x25 *
FF 222 444 666 888 (ANY 1 SUIT) c30

LIKE NUMBERS
FF 1111 1111 1111 (ANY LIKE NOS.) x25
11 DD 111 DDD 1111 (3 SUITS; ANY LIKE NOS.) c30

ADDITION: HEAVENLY 11s
FFFF 5555+6666=11 or FFFF 5555+6666=11 (1 OR 3 SUITS) x25
FFFF 4444+7777=11 or FFFF 4444+7777=11 (1 OR 3 SUITS) x25
FFFF 3333+8888=11 or FFFF 3333+8888=11 (1 OR 3 SUITS) x25

QUINTS — VALUES
22 333 4444 55555 (ANY 1 SUIT, THESE NOS. ONLY) .... X 45
11111 2222 33333 OR 11111 2222 33333 (1 OR 3 SUITS, ANY CONSEC. NOS.) X 45
FFFF NNNNN 11111 (ANY WIND, ANY NO.) .... X 45
FFFF DDDDD 11111 (ANY DRAGON, ANY NO.) .... X 45

CONSECUTIVE RUN
11 222 3333 444 55 OR 55 666 7777 888 99 (ANY 1 SUIT) .... X 25
* 111 2222 333 4444 (ANY 2 SUITS, 4 CONSEC. NOS.) .... X 25
* FFFF 1111 2222 DD OR FFFF 1111 2222 DD (1 OR 3 SUITS, ANY CONSEC. NOS.) X 25
* 11 22 111 222 3333 (3 SUITS, ANY CONSEC. NOS.) .... X 25
1111 22 22 22 3333 (ANY 3 CONSEC. NOS., PAIRS MIDDLE NO. ONLY) .... X 25
111 22 333 DDD DDD (ANY 3 CONSEC. NOS., NON-MATCHING DRAGONS) .... C 30

1 3 5 7 9
11 333 5555 777 99 (ANY 1 SUIT) .... X 25
111 3333 333 5555 OR 555 7777 777 9999 (ANY 2 SUITS) .... X 25
FFFF 1111 33 5555 OR FFFF 1111 33 5555 (1 OR 3 SUITS) .... X 25
FFFF 5555 77 9999 OR FFFF 5555 77 9999 (1 OR 3 SUITS) .... X 25
FF 1111 9999 DDDD OR FF 1111 9999 DDDD (1 OR 3 SUITS) .... X 25
11 333 DDDD 333 55 OR 55 777 DDDD 777 99 (3 SUITS) .... X 25
111 3 555 555 7 999 (ANY 2 SUITS) .... C 30

WINDS AND DRAGONS — VALUES
NNNN EEEE WWWW SS .... X 25
FF DDDD NEWS DDDD (ANY 2 DRAGONS) .... X 25
NNNN SSSS 111 111 (ANY 2 SUITS, PUNGS ANY LIKE ODD NO. ONLY) .... C 25
EEEE WWWW 222 222 (ANY 2 SUITS, PUNGS ANY LIKE EVEN NO. ONLY) .... C 25
FF DDDD DDDD DDDD .... X 25

3 6 9
3333 66 9999 DDDD (ANY 1 SUIT) .... X 25
FF 3333 6666 9999 OR FF 3333 6666 9999 (1 OR 3 SUITS) .... X 25
33 66 99 3333 3333 (3 SUITS, KONGS 3S, 6S, OR 9S) .... X 25
333 666 9999 9999 (3 SUITS, KONGS, 9S ONLY) .... C 25

SINGLES AND PAIRS
NN EE WW SS 11 11 22 (3 SUITS, THESE NOS. ONLY) .... C 50
FF 11 22 33 44 55 DD (ANY 1 SUIT, ANY 5 CONSEC. NOS.) .... C 50
FF 22 44 66 88 22 88 (ANY 2 SUITS, LAST PAIRS ONLY 2S AND 8S) .... C 50
11 33 55 77 99 11 11 (LAST 2 PAIRS ANY LIKE ODD NO.) .... C 50
FF 11 22 11 22 11 22 (ANY 2 CONSEC. NOS.) .... C 50
336 33669 336699 (ALL 3 SUITS) .... C 50
FF 2019 2020 2021 (ANY 3 CONSEC. YEARS IN 21ST CENTURY, 3 SUITS) .... C 75

Put the card under your rack.

Getting Tiles

There are five different ways to get tiles, some of which we've already covered: the deal and the Charleston. When the Charleston is complete, it's time for the next phase: actual play. This is the time when players pick, rack, discard, call, and exchange tiles for Jokers. Picking, Calling and Exchanging allow you to build your hands, and hopefully call out "Mah Jongg" before anyone else does.

Playing the Game

East, sometimes known as the dealer, begins the game. Remember: East has one more tile than the other players. East begins play by **discarding (throwing)** and naming the tile. (By the way, when we say "throw," we're not being literal. If you actually throw a tile, it's considered rude. Place your discarded tile faceup in the middle of the table.) Now everyone has 13 tiles. The playing field has been leveled.

> As you did in the Charleston, and as a Beginner, keep your unwanted tiles on the right side of your rack. This way you won't be confused about which tiles you do care about, and the game will keep moving along. When you become more comfortable with the game, you may decide on another way to denote unwanted tiles: have them upside down, placed in the center of the rack—no matter. You work out what you like and stick to it. The important thing is you come up with a system.

Picking

If no one "calls" the discarded tile to complete the grouping they need (we will get to that concept a bit later), play proceeds in a counterclockwise direction. (Remember, people to the right, walls to the left.)

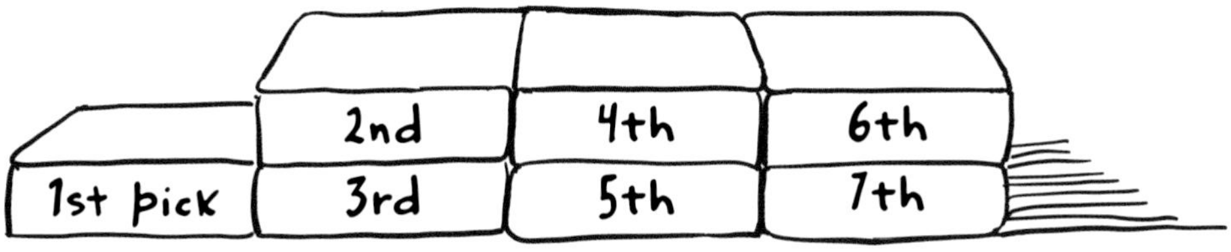

Tiles are picked in this order.

The next player on the right will pick the lower tile at the end of the wall that has just been dealt from. After that tile has been racked, and another discarded and named, play proceeds to the right. Tiles are picked from the top to the bottom layer of the wall, proceeding one stack at a time. Play continues to the right until someone calls for a discard or says "Mah Jongg," with 14 tiles matching a hand on the card. Sometimes no one wins by the time all the tiles have been picked—that's a **Wall Game**. Sounds rather simple, but skill, strategy and luck must all be on your side.

G&T Time:

Toby: Keep your tiles together! I can't stress this enough. Once you have organized the tiles, eliminate the space between the groups. If you leave a large gap, you're telling your story, but it's supposed to be your secret. If you have two tiles waaaay on the right of your rack, your opponents know that you're three tiles away from calling Mah Jongg. Likewise, if your opponent has two tiles to the far left and a big gap after that pair, you might just assume those two tiles are Jokers or a Pair. The less information you give, the better your chances of keeping your hand a mystery.

Gregg: I'm trying hard to get rid of the bad habits I developed along the way, and doing my best to make myself do what we're telling you to do. Get into good habits from the beginning: it's much easier that way.

Racking

When you pick your tile from the wall, place it in your rack on the hidden angled lip. This is "**racking**": your tile resting on the lip of your rack. Tapping your tile on your card or on top of your rack does not count. And don't be an overly quick picker if you're playing with people who are not as experienced as you are. Pick and rack at the same speed as others.

Discarding

Once you've racked your tile, it's time to discard. Pick a tile from the unwanted tile section of your rack, and discard it by naming it and placing it on the table. Make sure you're discarding the one you want—keep unwanted tiles in a special part of the rack.

When you're discarding, again, be careful you have the right tile. If you say the full name of a tile, or if it touches the table, it has been discarded. If you realize you made a mistake, it's too late. Of course, every player has done this, but a rule's a rule. So get into the right habit now. Double-check before you discard, and make sure to say the right name. If the next player discards the same tile, "same" can be said rather than the tile name. This is also the case when a Joker is discarded. Sadly, a discarded Joker can't be claimed, ever. That tile is dead.

Calling for a Tile

A lot of thinking must happen before you call to claim a discard. First and foremost is: what kind of hand are you going for? And are you playing an Exposed hand or a Concealed one?

As discussed in Chapter 4, there are two main types of hands: Exposed and Concealed. Look to the far right of the hands on our card. You will see a red **X** or a **C**. **X** = Exposed; C = **C**oncealed or **C**an't **C**all.

If you're playing an Exposed hand, you may call for a tile to complete a group of three or more identical tiles as seen in a separate gouping of the card. If you're playing a Concealed (closed) hand and a tile you need gets thrown, you can't call unless it is the 14th tile you need to complete a Mah Jongg. That's why these Concealed hands garner higher points. They're a greater challenge, but don't you want bragging rights?

When playing an Exposed hand, and you need a tile to complete a group of three or more identical tiles, if that tile has just been discarded (and the next player has not racked their pick), you can say "wait" "call" or "take." These will be some of the most obvious things to say, but lots of other words are used, too. Even if you're just thinking about it, you can say those words to give yourself a moment. You can change your mind—there's no penalty. Once you pick up a tile and place it on your rack, that tile's yours.

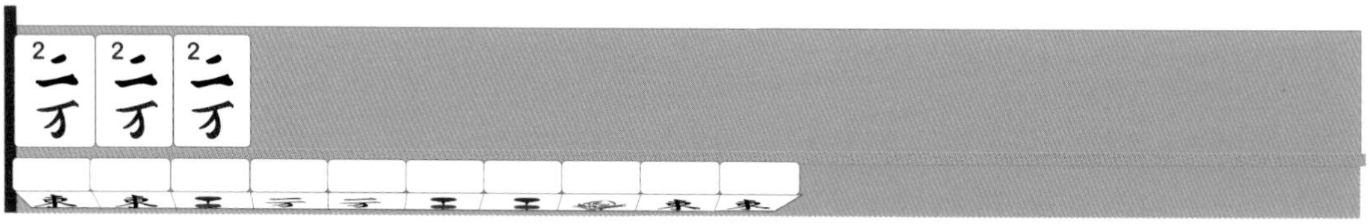

One Pung is exposed, but it could be for lots of hands.
That said, players will start trying to guess what you're doing.

When you pick up a discard, it's best to first place the tile on top of your rack and put your other tiles in that grouping around it. This means you are exposing three (Pung) four (Kong) or even five (Quint) tiles. Now all the players can see what you have exposed, and they might start to figure out what hand you're playing.

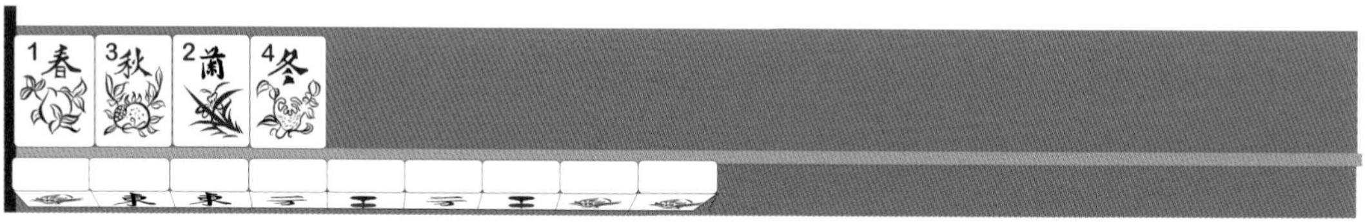

This could be one of eight hands. You still have not revealed too much.

But don't rush to call for a tile: we've seen new players do this, exposing a grouping on their rack while still having no idea which hand they're going for. Once you've called and shown your group of tiles, and you've discarded, you're committed to using those tiles; you can't add to or take away from them. This is your exposure. Before you discard, you can fiddle with the number of tiles you're exposing. (This happens sometimes when you're between hands but you know you need a tile.) You can change the number of tiles in your exposure until you discard, but you'll be giving other players information about your hand.

What if you're not sure about which hands to play, but both need the same Pung or Kong? Call for the tile. You can decide on the hand later.

A few important words about grouping. Some years the Card calls for six Flowers in a hand, but on the Card they appear: FFF FFF. See the space between the Fs? You can call for a Flower if you can complete a grouping, in this case three.

Now this is why correct racking is key: as we wrote before, when you have just picked a tile from the wall, until your tile is actually racked, any player can call the last discard. If the picked tile has already been racked, that discard is dead for the rest for the game. It's to your advantage to rack as soon as possible to prevent other players from calling discards. If someone calls a tile and you still have your picked tile in your hand, you have to return it to the wall, even if you've seen it. (And it's awfully painful to put back a tile you need—or a Joker—we know because we've been there. Now we rack quickly!)

It's really important to know when to call for a discard. You know you can only call when you can complete a grouping, and you're playing an Exposed hand. But what about the timing of your call? Should you call the first time a tile comes out? It all depends on what tile it is: a Flower or something else. Say the game has just started, and you need four Flowers for the hand you are playing. You have one, you're lucky enough to have two Jokers, and someone discards a Flower. You're anxious to get in on the game. Should you call that tile? No. Remember: there are eight Flowers. You have a good chance of getting more of them yourself. Exposing groups with a few Jokers allows other players a chance to get those Jokers (more about that later in this chapter).

Let's say you need a Kong of **8 Craks**; you have one of them and two Jokers. Should you call for the first one discarded? Maybe—depending on how your hand is coming along. What if you need a Pung of **7 Craks** and you have one tile and a Joker, and it's early in the game? The first **7 Crak** is discarded. Should you call it? You can, but it's early, and you may actually get another **7 Crak** yourself, allowing you to call for the third one without using a Joker. But if you are a tile away from Mah Jongg, call using your Jokers. You're trying to beat the clock in order to win.

Also, anyone can call a discard, even if they're not the next player to draw. Once someone calls for a tile, exposes their group and discards, the player on the right (counterclockwise) is the next to pick. So sometimes a player (or players) will lose their turn if another player calls a tile.

Remember: you can (almost) never call a discarded tile if it's for a single or a pair. But there's an exception: for Mah Jongg, you can call for a Single, or the tile needed to complete a Pair. Your 14th tile, your Mah Jongg tile, can be called no matter what.

What happens when two players call for the same tile? The person who comes next in the order of play gets it unless another player has started to expose their tiles. But if a player calls the tile for Mah Jongg, they get it. Mah Jongg beats everything. Note: it's USUALLY not about who calls first, but rather the position of your seat. And if *two* people want a tile for Mah Jongg, it goes to the person next in the order of play, and that person wins. There are no ties.

> Remember: a discarded tile, one that has touched the table or has been fully named, is a discarded tile. But sometimes players make mistakes. What happens when a player miscalls a tile? This happens all the time. Suppose a player puts out a 2 Bam but calls out a 2 Crak. Another player might notice and correct the name of the miscalled tile. Or a player might put the miscalled tile in front of the player who threw the tile. That gives them an opportunity to correct themselves and pay better attention. If no one notices at all until later, the game simply continues. Once a tile hits the table, it is discarded, even if misidentified. The player can't take it back. There's a caveat: if a tile has been miscalled and another person says "Mah Jongg" based on that call, the game ceases. And, by the way, a tile can't be called by another player for an exposure unless it's properly named.

Joker Exchange

Here's one of the most exciting parts of the game: the Joker Exchange! It's the last of the five ways you'll get tiles. The moment an exposure is placed on top of the rack, see if a Joker has been used, and if all the natural (non-Joker) tiles are visible anywhere else on the table. If a Joker is part of a Pung, Kong or Quint, and all the tiles can't be accounted for, the Joker is "alive." Look in your own hand to see if you have that tile. If you do, when it's your turn, first pick from the wall and rack your tile (or call for the most recent discard and make the exposures). Then say "tile please" or "Exchange," and hand your matching tile to the person with the exposure. Don't do the Exchange yourself. The player will take the tile from your hand and exchange it for the exposed Joker. Then you discard an unwanted tile. This move can be the difference between winning and losing. Whenever a Joker is used for an Exposure, and it's alive, be on the lookout for the natural tile. By the way, the player with the Joker may get the natural tile themself and exchange it for their own Joker later. You can do Joker Exchanges even if you're playing a Concealed hand.

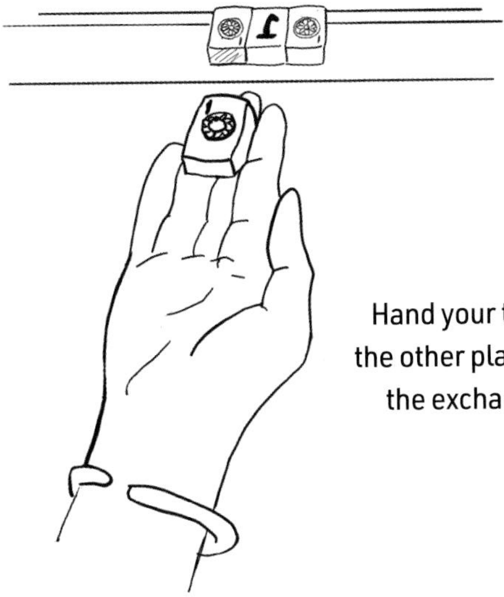

Hand your tile to the other player for the exchange.

Suppose a player makes an exposure of Quints with three Jokers. You have two of those tiles. When your turn comes around, pick and rack. Then say "Exchange." Hand your two matching tiles to the player whose tiles are exposed, your tiles will be exchanged for the Jokers, and you'll have two Jokers for your own use. Happy Day!! This can change the game for you. You can exchange any number of tiles on your turn, even with multiple players.

Let's say another player mistakenly threw a tile that could have been exchanged for a Joker. No one can call that tile and do the Exchange. That tile is dead, and nobody can use it. You can call it and use it in your own hand though, for your own exposure if you need it, but you can't call it and exchange it for someone else's Joker.

There is a scenario where you can be tricky. Suppose you only need one tile to complete a Pair for Mah Jongg, but you have a natural tile for an exposed Joker. If you have Pungs or Kongs in your hand, make the Exchange. Throw one of the tiles from your Pung or Kong as a discard, using the Joker you just took to replace that tile. Hopefully people won't know you're just one tile away from Mah Jongg. Don't let them know how close you are to a win.

When someone doesn't exchange a tile, very often players will comment and even reprimand the player. It can be assumed they missed the opportunity. Never comment! You don't know if this was deliberate, or an error. Maybe they erred, or maybe they are working on a Singles and Pairs hand? You just don't know. And if *you* missed the exchange, soldier on.

Calling for Mah Jongg

There are a few ways to acquire your last tile for Mah Jongg. You might pick it from the wall. You might have the tile for another player's Joker exposure, in which case, on your turn, you pick a needed tile, you rack, exchange for the Joker and then announce Mah Jongg using that Joker. Or you might call for your 14th tile. When you call a tile for Mah Jongg, follow our advice and take a deep breath. Do you really have Mah Jongg? Do you have the right number of tiles? Is it really the tile you need? Take an extra moment and ask yourself these questions. Once you call Mah Jongg and expose your tiles, if you don't have it right, it's "Mah Jongg in error," and you're dead. Just call for the tile, and once you've double-checked, you can say "Mah Jongg."

Suppose someone else calls for Mah Jongg. Don't expose your tiles or throw your tiles onto the table. Verify the Mah Jongg's correct. You don't want to forfeit your hand if someone else has made a mistake. If you've already thrown in your tiles and it's "Mah Jongg in error" you too are "dead" and no longer in the game.

The Last Wall or the Hot Wall

The Hot Wall is the wall that East (the dealer) held back at the beginning of the game. Remember that far back?!? It might be made of any number of stacks between two and twelve. The tiles are pushed out just the same as every other wall. The game ends when all tiles have been picked from the wall and the final tile is discarded, or when a player has 14 tiles that match a hand on the card and calls Mah Jongg. In the Hot Wall, it is considered good form to play as defensively as you can. If you see an opponent with two or more exposures, there's a good chance you know what they're playing. Try your best not to give that player what you think they need. On the other hand, if you know you're too far away to win, throw Jokers as discards if you have them. Remember, a Joker down is down forever, and no one can take it.

Example:
A player has two exposures:

3 Dot 3 Dot 3 Dot 3 Dot 6 Crak 6 Crak 6 Crak 6 Crak

You might surmise, correctly, that they are playing the second hand in **3 6 9**, the one on the right. If you have a 9 Bam, you might "destroy" your hand to hold onto what you

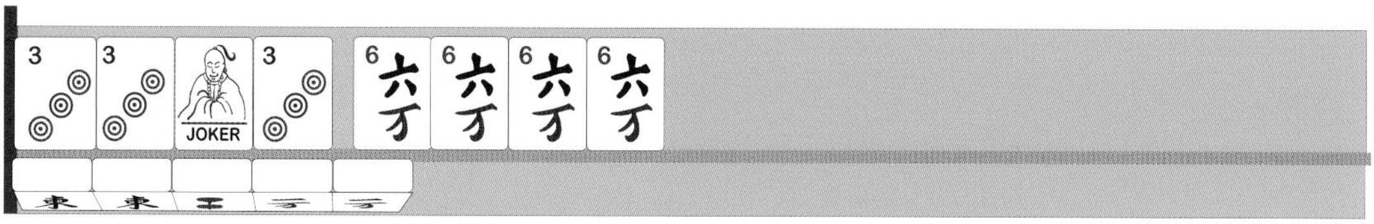

Two Kongs exposed. What hand could this be?

think this player needs. You wouldn't throw the **9 Bam**, nor would you throw a Flower. Sacrifice something else from your hand, hoping nobody wins, rather than throw a tile another player needs. One of the great tenets of Mah Jongg is that if you can't win, you don't want anyone to win. You have to channel your killer instincts to play this game!

Try your best to discard what might be important tiles (Flowers, Soaps) before you get to the Hot Wall. How easy it is for someone to have finally acquired everything they need except for a Flower, or a Soap. Be on guard—don't throw them. Hope for a Wall Game.

When all the tiles have been taken from the wall, and the last tile has been discarded, and nobody has won, it's a **Wall Game**.

A Few More Words

There are a few ways a hand can go **dead**. If a player has too many or too few tiles, that's that. You can call a player's hand dead if their exposures are wrong, they have too many or too few tiles, or if you know the only hand they are going for can't happen based on discards. If they're playing a hand needing two Pairs, and enough of the tiles have been discarded so the hand is impossible, that hand is dead. It's to your advantage to call someone's hand dead: you then get more picks from the wall.

Sometimes a player has two exposures, both having Jokers in them; and the second exposure proves the hand is incorrect, thus dead. Jokers can be exchanged from that first exposure, but not the second. It was the second one that proved the hand dead, so those Jokers are not available (sigh).

Calling Mah Jongg is exciting, and it can be even more so if "**self-picked**," i.e., you pick it yourself from the wall. Everyone has to pay you double the value on the hand. If you get Mah Jongg because of a discard, the discarder pays you double. And if your hand is Jokerless, you get double, too.

Summary

After tiles have been washed, walls built, tiles dealt and the Charleston completed, play starts. East begins the game with a discard of one of their 14 tiles. Everyone now has 13 tiles. The next player to the right will pick, rack and discard. During the game, tiles can be acquired in three ways: picking from the wall, calling a discard to complete a grouping, and by a Joker Exchange. You can only exchange a tile on your turn after you have picked and racked a tile. You can never call a discarded Joker. Remember: to call a tile, the hand you're playing must have an X at the end of its line on the card, unless it is the final tile you need for Mah Jongg on a Concealed (C) hand. You can only call for a Single or a Pair (that includes NEWS and a year, such as 2021) for Mah Jongg, whether the hand is Exposed (X) or Concealed (C). The first player to match a hand on the card with 14 tiles is declared the winner. Sometimes all the tiles in the wall have been used and the last tile discarded and there's no winner: that's a wall game.

Quiz

1 Can you call for a single tile for Mah Jongg?
2 What's the only tile to throw at the end of the game if you know you can't win?
3 Which comes first, picking or racking?
4 If you click your tile on top of your rack, is that considered racking?
5 When can you call a discard for a concealed hand?
6 When two players want the same discard, who can claim the tile?
7 True or False: The moment someone declares Mah Jongg, throw in your tiles and proceed to the next game.
8 True or False: It's always good to remind players to rack their tiles.
9 True or False: You can use a Joker in a Pair when it's for Mah Jongg.
10 Can you call a tile and then exchange it in an exposed hand?
11 When might you not exchange a tile for a Joker?

12 True or False: Always point out a missed exchange in an exposure.

13 How many tiles does a player need to complete a Mah Jongg?

14 If a player wants to pass three tiles on the optional Over, and the player across from them wants to pass one tile, how many tiles are passed by each of them?

15 True or False: You can NEVER call a single or a pair for Mah Jongg.

Answers

1 Yes.

2 A Joker is the only safe tile to throw. No one can ever call for it.

3 Picking comes first.

4 No, racking only refers to a tile resting on the hidden lower lip of the rack.

5 When you are playing a Concealed hand, you can only call a discarded tile for Mah Jongg.

6 Usually the next player in the rotation or the player who needs the tile for Mah Jongg gets it. Mah Jongg beats everything, and if two players need the same tile to win, the next person in the rotation gets it unless someone else has started an exposure. There are no ties in Mah Jongg.

7 False. Wait until that "winning" hand has been checked; there might have been a mistake.

8 False. You might want to take advantage of their pokiness and think about your own tiles.

9 False. A Joker can never be used for a Single or as part of a Pair.

10 No; once a tile is discarded it can no longer be called and exchanged for a Joker. You may, however, call it and use it in an exposure of your own.

11 If you only need a Single tile or a tile for a Pair.

12 False.

13 14 tiles are needed for Mah Jongg.

14 One, because the lowest number of tiles is the number of tiles passed.

15 False. You can <u>only</u> call for a single or a pair for Mah Jongg.

Chapter 8

Basic and Advanced Strategy

Is Mah Jongg a game of luck or a game of skill? You'll hear this debated for the rest of your Mah Jongg life. The truth is, if an unskilled player gets five Jokers, they will probably lose. If a seasoned player starts out with a complete hand shy of one or two tiles, and those two tiles never come up, they'll lose, too. You need skill and luck to be a winner. Some wise people have looked at the odds of winning a game of Mah Jongg, and say that if you play against people at your skill level, all things (and Jokers) being equal, you can expect to win one in five games. Wall games will average the same. So instead of just thinking about winning, players need to develop their skills to not let others win. At

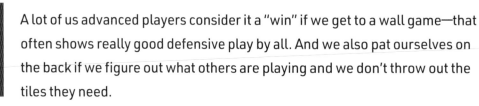

a tournament players gain points for wall games, and points are subtracted when they throw the winning tile. Figuring out others' hands and playing defensively are important parts of Mah Jongg strategy. This chapter will help you accomplish whatever is in your control.

A lot of us advanced players consider it a "win" if we get to a wall game—that often shows really good defensive play by all. And we also pat ourselves on the back if we figure out what others are playing and we don't throw out the tiles they need.

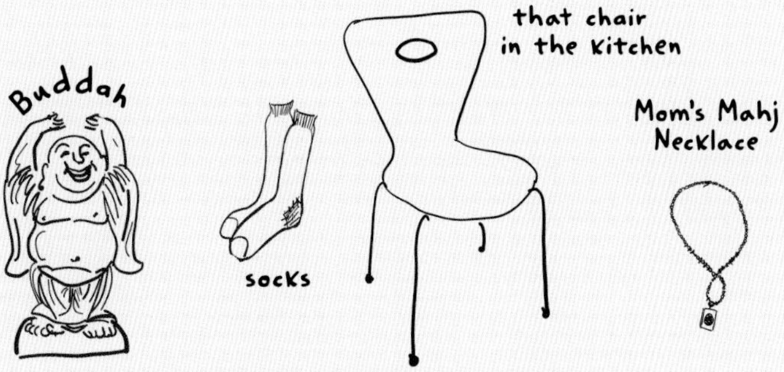

G&T Time:

Things people find lucky in Mah Jong

Toby: Luck is important. Players have good luck charms and rituals. One woman keeps a little figurine on her rack, her Mah Jongg talisman. Another woman has her "song." She sings it silently MOST of the time and knows this is why she wins. Some have lucky socks, others, lucky chairs. When my goddaughter turned 7, I gave her a chunky, sparkly gold Mah Jongg set. My dear friend, her mother, called me to say, "It's my lucky set!" I conjure the Mah Jongg gods. Sometimes they love me and sometimes they don't.

Gregg: We all know people who are just plain lucky. Jokers fly into their hands when they need them most. One woman at a tournament bought a bracelet, and she won the round. She bought another bracelet, and won again. She ended up with a lot of bracelets and a big check for winning the tournament! Sometimes I wonder if it's the chair the player is sitting in: I have gone so far as to tie a ribbon around the "lucky" chair after games to see if it gives a player the same luck the next time. (My husband keeps removing it, so the scientific

study has not yet been completed.) There certainly are some Feng Shui principles that you can use, but Lady Luck is notoriously fickle—and she certainly has her favorites. If for some reason you're not among them at the moment, you need to have bagful of tricks to help to increase your chance of saying our favorite words: "Mah Jongg."

All of this being said, let's see how you can be the best player you can be.

The Card

Know your NMJL Card! This is the best way to increase your chances of winning. Know it backwards and forwards. We have touched on this, but we can't emphasize it enough.

EXERCISE

Lay out all of your tiles face-up and organize them by number and suit. When you get your Card, start with the first section, the upper left. Make every hand in that category, and try to make every version of the hands. What does that mean?!? Using our Card as an example, let's take the first hand. You can use Dots, Bams and Craks for Line 1. Let's say you used Bams and Dots. Make it again using another combination, and then again to make it the last way. This will give you a physical memory of making the hand, which will be helpful when you're playing. Not only is Mah Jongg a visual game, it's also tactile. Seeing and making hands helps you embrace all the possibilities it might offer. Focus on one section a day. Too much and your head will be spinning. Do this with every hand in every section on the Card.

Every year the NMJL creates new hands that break the rules. Read the information in the parentheses. This is key. The hands aren't always easy to understand. If something is confusing, you can turn to online groups that will help you figure out the hand. You won't be the only one confused—we promise.

Some players call for an exposure, only to belatedly realize that it's a concealed hand. They're stuck, and they have to use it. So, when you first get the Card, underline or highlight the concealed hands to ensure you're not making this error.

The Charleston or the Passes

One of the best strategies is to collect from the beginning. Say you have no Jokers, no Flowers, no pairs. Hmmm.... Your inclination might be to assume you're doomed. But no! There is always something to hang your hat on. If you have two Winds, collect every Wind you get. We've done this and wound up with as many as eight Wind tiles by the end of the Charleston!

If you have a White Dragon, collect every related year numbers that come your way. By the end of the passes you may just have a solid hand.

It's not necessarily about choosing a specific hand, but rather about being fluid. Mah Jongg is like life. We think we're headed in a nice, neat direction, and along comes a big change that forces us to reinvent, to survive and thrive. Sometimes one tile can make you realize you can go in a whole new direction.

G&T Time:

Gregg: Here's a trick I like. When I'm dealt tiles, and I have a pair that I know makes no sense whatsoever for any hand I'd play, I pass one of them in my first Charleston pass, and I hold onto the other. I often find that later in the game, the same kind of tile will be thrown, another player will call it, and when it's my turn I'll get to do the Joker Exchange. Of course this doesn't work all the time, but it can be helpful. And every little bit helps.
Toby: Sometimes you see the same tiles go round and round. You think nothing new will come your way, but someone chooses one hand over another and suddenly new discards are flying around. Keep your focus.

Play Begins

The Rack

Set up your rack. We've a few suggestions. Have tiles organized in a way you like. Put your discards in a certain spot—many of us leave them on the far right, ready to discard without thinking about them. When playing, keep your tiles together! You can leave teensy gaps to keep organized, but when you leave three tiles far to the right of your rack, others will most likely guess that you're four tiles away from Mah Jongg.

When it's your turn to pick, separate your tiles and drop your picked tile into the middle of your rack. Close the gap up again, and discard. Then rearrange your tiles. No one will know if this pick was helpful to you. Remember, even the placement of your tiles tells your story. You want to keep your story a secret.

Calling for Tiles

Many advanced players don't call a tile when it's the first one out if they're going to have to use a few Jokers. They'll wait for the second time it's discarded. IF you call for a discard, try to wait until you only need to use one of your Jokers. (This works with

Pungs). Of course there are always exceptions: if you're one tile away from Mah Jongg, and it's early in the game, go ahead and call it using Jokers. Set yourself up early to get your needed Mah Jongg tile as soon as it comes out. Yes, you might be helping out other players, but you're ready for the "Mah Jongg **pounce**!" A pounce enables you to call for any needed tile the first time it's discarded.

The NMJL will not allow you to call for a tile if the tile's been incorrectly named. If you need a 4 Bam, and the tile's been discarded but it's been called a 4 Dot, you have to get the player to correctly name it and then you can call it.

We all make mistakes, and we might say "Call" or "Pause" to indicate we want a discard—but what if we realize we can't pick it up? We cover for ourselves by saying: "Oh, that was my last game" or "I forgot I changed hands." We don't let anyone know we need that tile. But if another player calls but doesn't pick it up, and you have that same tile, get rid of it right away. You may not get a tile exchange, but you might be preventing the other player from getting Mah Jongg. They might not be able to call for it the first time, but by discarding the tile right away as a tactical move, you might be able to prevent them from winning.

Calling for an Exposure

When you call for an exposure…stop! Make absolutely sure you need that tile. Once you place it on your rack, it's yours. Be careful to expose the correct number of tiles before you discard. It's nearly impossible to save yourself if you've made an error. If you realize you can't win, play defensively. If a tile's already been placed on the table, try throwing the same one. If there's a Joker exposed, try to replace it and then throw the Joker. No one can ever call for a Joker.

Discarding Tiles

One strategy we all love is "**Joker bait**," otherwise known as saving a pair you don't need. Let's say you're playing a hand and you have a pair you don't need. IF you can wait long enough, you might just be able to get a Joker! This often works best if you wait to discard until there are about 50 tiles left to pick, 25 stacks. When people may be getting desperate, they'll call a tile they might not otherwise have called. Say you have a pair of 8 Bams. At the right time, discard an 8 Bam. One of the other players says "Call." The player places the 8 Bam with his or her own 8 Bam and also exposes a Joker. When your turn comes around, pick and rack your tile and then exchange the other half of your pair (your **8 Bam**) to earn the exposed Joker. This is also commonly done with Flowers. But Flowers are tricky. So many people have Flowers they don't need, and another player whose turn comes before yours might be able to do the exchange. And remember: if you throw a Flower too late in the game and someone calls, it just might be their Mah Jongg tile.

> Many beginning players hold onto Flowers hoping to use them to get Jokers later in the game, when another player calls for a Flower discard and exposes Flowers and a Joker or two. This ploy can work, but most advanced players will discard Flowers right at the beginning of the game. They don't want to run the risk of discarding them later and giving another player Mah Jongg.

We know that no tile has more value than another. That being said, Flowers are typically used in the most hands on the card, making them quite desirable. And don't forget, although "all tiles are equal," the Soap has two roles. The last thing you want to do is throw this tile at the end of the game, giving it to a player who needed it for the Zero or Dragon. If you don't need these tiles, discard them early.

G&T Time:

Toby: I'll often throw the same tile that just went out. I'll think either no one wants it or they can't call it. Or they might have to use the only Joker they have, and this might stop them from calling for another group in their hand.

Gregg: I love trying to throw people off when I only need one tile. Let's say my exposures indicate I could be playing one of two hands. If I have Jokers that can cover, I throw a tile associated with the hand I'm actually playing. More times than not, people think I'm playing the other hand and throw the tile I need.

Proactive Discarding

It's sometimes good to discard before you call tiles. Say you're working on a **LIKE NUMBER** hand, and you have a tile right below that number or right above. Throw that tile before you call for your like number. People won't remember that you threw it (in all probability), so they won't know if you're doing a run or another variation. If at all possible when you're one tile away from Mah Jongg, don't throw a Joker. Perhaps you just need one tile to win for a single or a pair, and you pick up a Joker: don't discard it. Instead throw a tile that you can cover for using your Joker. You won't get a Jokerless hand, but you may well get a win—nobody will guess you need a pair or a single.

Other Player's Moves

When a player says "Call," watch where they take their tiles from in their own rack. Sneaky. If they take them from the middle of the rack, and the exposure is four Flowers, and there's a hand where Flowers are in the middle, you can often guess which hand they're playing. Another example: If a player puts out five tiles, most years it's one of the **QUINT** hands. There are many indicators to help you figure out what someone is doing. Once an exposure is made, be extra careful to see what they're discarding.

When a tile's called and a Joker (or two) is exposed, the first thing to do is verify that the tile is alive. Are they all on the table? It is soooo easy to miss a tile exchange. It's entirely possible to make several Joker Exchanges <u>during</u> your turn. (You have to wait your turn, pick and rack your tile, and then ask for the Exchange.)

As a player, you need to be able to guess which hands other people are playing. On some cards, just the number of Flowers exposed will give you an idea of which hands are being played. If there are two exposures, you have even more information. If it's early in the game, get rid of any tiles you think that player may need, but <u>don't</u> do this late in the game. You might very well be giving them Mah Jongg, and the other players will be annoyed with you.

Remember, it's your job to play defensively. It's also your job to listen and look. Players will often miscall a tile. This isn't done with malice, it just happens. You must pay attention. If you miss a tile, the onus is on you.

BACKUP PLANS

Power Hands: The most powerful strategy of all is the Backup. You're going for a hand that has a pair or pairs that you don't have yet. Suddenly these pairs have been discarded and you're lost. Don't despair. Several hands on the card don't require singles and pairs. We call these Jokers galore or power hands. Look at the card. Maybe a **CONSECUTIVE RUN** might work, or even a **QUINT**. Know your backups.

Let's say you're going for a **SINGLES AND PAIRS** hand in the bottom right corner. You're close. You can feel the tingling in your hands. You're ready to win. You're holding your breath. Only two tiles to go…. Well, the third tile of one of your pairs goes out, and all hopes are dashed. Fine. Pick yourself up and go for a hand from that category. If you were going for a **3 6 9** hand, just go up to the **3 6 9** category and work on something there. Do your best to save yourself. Don't give up.

G&T Time:

Toby: Suppose you have a great hand right after the passes, and then you sit. And you sit. And you sit. Nothing seems to be happening. My mother used to say, "I think I have a partner…." It's very likely that two or more of the players need the same tiles. If another player calls, and you have their tiles, you will be able to snag a Joker or two from them. You might be able to switch to another hand.

Gregg: This happens more often than not. That's why you need a backup plan.

The End of the Game

The Hot Wall. This is the last wall to be pushed out, and it's one of the places people have "**house rules**." These are rules specific to that group; they've made them up, but all abide by them. During play on the Hot Wall, it is crucial not to discard the tiles that you think another player needs. Some players "throw" their game, and break up their own hand. They toss tiles that they're quite sure no one needs. At the very end, if you know you're too many tiles away from a possible win, the only tile to throw is a Joker. We suggest you think about this during the last twenty or so tiles of the game. Remember: your goal is to win, but if you can't win you don't want anyone else to win. So give up the dream and break up your hand.

G&T Time:

Toby: I can't tell you how many times I have seen someone toss the last tile, name it, and then a player triumphantly calls "MAH JONGG!" Example: I was playing with a lovely group of women, and at the end of the game, one of the women tossed her tile. She did not name it. I said that she needed to name her tile. Rolling her eyes, she announced the tile's name. Me: Call for MAH JONGG! You just never know....

Gregg: I had one of those exciting moments happen to me. I only needed a Green Dragon. I had three Jokers, but I'd given up on the win. An experienced player, knowing there were three Greens on the table, threw the Green Dragon and I said "Mah Jongg!" She was so upset with herself because she could've thrown a Joker. I, of course, was THRILLED!!

Notice what others are discarding. Is it all evens? Odds? Are all of the Winds going out? I always want to try and throw "safe" tiles. Many advanced players pay attention to Winds and look around to see if they might be part of other players' hands. If everyone is discarding them, start holding onto them during the last third of the game. You can probably safely discard them at the end if you don't have any Jokers.

Quiz

1. Why would you save a pair that you don't need?
2. Which tile should I toss if I can't win at the end of the game?
3. When should you start to break up your hand?

Answers

1. To try and get a Joker when someone calls for that tile.
2. A Joker or any other tiles you are confident nobody wants, often Winds.
3. Break up your hand when it seems you won't win and you're in the Hot Wall.

Chapter 9

Three-Person Play

We all know that Mah Jongg requires four players. That being said, someone is always busy at work, ill or heading out of town. The League has devised a way for three people to play, knowing this is a frequent problem.

The National Mah Jongg League Rules for Three-Person Play

Four walls are built. Standard. Right? Then East begins the "deal," taking four tiles. Just like we have learned, each player takes the next four tiles until all have three piles of four. East takes the top first and third tiles, and the next two players take one tile each from the end of the wall. Here's the surprise: there's no Charleston! East discards the first tile and the game begins.

G&T Time:

Toby: We name the empty chair, so it seems as if we have four players. We fondly call her Gerty, the name of the mother of one of our players.
Gregg: We call ours Mia (MIA) because she's missing in action. She's very popular because she's always available and she never complains.

She's with us in spirit.

Table Rules for the Game

Now, "**table rules,**" or "house rules," are made-up rules. Groups agree to play in a certain manner. Any deviation from the NMJL standard isn't endorsed by the League. Many teachers encourage the Charleston, especially for beginning players, because it helps them shape their hands. But they know it's not the "right" way to do things.

Here's the way most of us handle the situation. Three of us set up the four walls. East takes the first four tiles and deals the next four to Mia (or Gerty), placing them in front of the rack. The deal continues in this manner until all players have 13 tiles and East has 14.

Then Mia's tiles are lined up, one layer only, 13 in a row. Passes begin. Tiles are left (passed) to the left of that line of tiles, and removed (taken away) from the right end, just like service at a dinner party. This continues until all passes are completed. R O L L O R: Right, Over, Left and Left, Over, Right. Even the Optional Pass can be made, with the player across from Mia taking any tiles from her assortment. If a Joker's passed it can be kept, but since these rules are made up, your group can decide if they want to exchange the Joker for another tile using the honor system. After the Charleston, Mia's tiles are added to the wall, at the end closest to the table's center, and will be the first ones picked by the actual players. Caveat: That wall will look different, because the end will be straight, not the stair-step we're used to seeing.

When you play with only two others, you increase your chances of getting Jokers and winning, so it's very exciting. Try hands you might be "afraid" to go for under other circumstances.

Chapter 10

Etiquette and Table Rules

Once you feel comfortable enough to play, you'll have to know Mah Jongg etiquette and table rules. There's a difference: etiquette is consistent from group to group, and table rules differ from table to table, and can vary depending on who's East. Take your etiquette with you, and you won't alienate any potential friends. And always ask about the table rules.

Etiquette

Etiquette in games, like in life, helps people get along. Given that Mah Jongg is a wonderful way to forge new friendships and sustain existing ones, the last thing you want to do is to offend anyone at the table. Following is our short course: Mah Jongg Etiquette 101. Often, students tell us that others who weren't our students have "bad habits." We always want to be our best selves when we play Mah Jongg!

When you're getting ready to host, here are a few tips. To start: Do not pull out a set that you're not sure has the correct number of tiles. Check it before your friends come over. And make sure your set is clean—nobody wants to play with a set that looks or feels horrible. Offer water and other drinks, and easy-to-eat foods.

Hard sourballs...
peppermint...
and licorice

Wrapped candies and licorice are always a good idea.

Make sure to "introduce" all of the Flowers, Dragons and 1 Bams to the players. Many sets are unique, and people don't want to make mistakes that could have been avoided with a "Pleased to meet you" exercise. Make sure your Jokers are obvious.

Have side tables where players can put drinks, money or candies. You only need two, placed at opposite corners of the game table. It is very important to keep the playing surface uncluttered—just tiles, racks and cards on the table.

When it comes to music, we keep a silent atmosphere, but it's your group's choice. It's very difficult for many of us to concentrate on the game when there are distractions. If there's music, think about soft and instrumental.

There are three no-no's everyone should know about.

Have small tables where players can place their drink glasses.

#1: **No cell phones.** Need we say another word?

#2: **Never touch another player's tiles or rack, even when making a Joker exchange.** Doing so is an invasion of that player's space. If you take your tile and exchange it for someone else's Joker, it's possible you'll knock down or expose their other tiles. Instead, hand your tile to the player and ask for their Joker.

#3: **It's a matter of courtesy not to comment on tiles that have been thrown, or, even more importantly, what's not been thrown.** If you're collecting Winds, for example, the last thing you want is for another player to say, "Someone must be collecting Winds." Keep your tile comments to yourself.

Your rack and card should be as close to you as possible. Your personal space is in front of you. If your elbows or hands rest in the corners of the table, you're in the "space" of others, and it can be very annoying. Make sure you respect your fellow players.

When you push out your wall, make sure you do so at a 45-degree angle. This way the tiles are equally visible to and reachable by everyone. We have seen many a player push out their wall an inch or two, creating a problem for the other players. When the wall is short, move it closer to the table's center.

Rack your tile when you pick it up, placing it onto the angled inner ledge of your rack. Tapping your tile on the rack—or worse, keeping it in your hand—does not qualify as "racking." Any other player would still have the right to call the previous discard.

This leads us to the next bit of etiquette: Don't grab and rack tiles faster than the other players. If you're an intermediate player and you're with a beginner, slow your pace down a bit. Allow newer players time to think. You needed it when you were just starting, so accord others that same respect. And if you realize you've racked at warp speed without thinking, and another player wants the discard, be polite and put the tile back.

When you're thinking about picking up a discarded tile, say so. Some of us have been known to respond to an "Um" or an "Ah," but in a game like this, there are plenty of "um" and "ahs" not related to tile calling. Many actual words can and should be used to stop the game when you're thinking about a tile. Here are just a few: "wait," "stop," "let me see," "hold," "give me a minute," or one of our favorites, "pause." Any of these make it clear you're thinking about the discard. Nothing else does. The moment one of these words is said, the game stops. If you decide you want it, say "call." Otherwise play resumes.

Most of us have been known to let our minds wander, even while at the Mah Jongg table. Sometimes a player discards, and the next player doesn't do anything. It's hard to know if they're thinking about the discard or just lost in thought. After a few seconds, gently ask: "Are you thinking about that tile?" That'll alert the player it's their turn.

> Don't be the person holding up the game. Yes, sometimes it's hard to know which direction to go in, but always making the right decision at the Mah Jongg table is impossible. Yes, you can delay play from time to time, but don't do it a lot. Other players won't like it.

Make sure to properly annunciate your discard. If a tile is misnamed by a player, point to the tile so they can read it, or correct them in a gentle manner if the game is going quickly. And remember, it's always up to you to listen and look!

There are times when a player is obviously much slower than the others. If you're playing together on a regular basis, and you think others may be bothered as well, bring up the pace of play at the beginning of the game. Perhaps you might say you think everyone is ready to try to speed things up a bit, and see how others feel. But don't focus on the slow player. Listen to the others. What's most important is friendship, not how many games you finish in an afternoon.

You shouldn't declare your hand **dead**, even to end your own misery about your bad hand. It's up to the other players to notice you've made an impossible exposure or two, and they must call your hand dead. If no one knows you can't win, just play as defensively as you can.

Calling another player's hand dead is tricky, and it can be upsetting. Remember, you can only call a hand dead based on the exposure(s) and discard(s), not what's in your hand. If you do call a hand dead, be kind. Many players feel embarrassed by mistakes, especially public ones.

The Mah Jongg table is a place we can complain about bad hands, lack of Jokers, wrong decisions...but don't do it all the time. If players moan a lot, it cuts down on everyone else's fun. Many of us turn to Mah Jongg to escape our worries and enjoy time together. Do your best to limit your conversation to tile washing and wall building time.

One of the unique aspects of Mah Jongg is that when a player wins, we all get to see the winning hand—but many of us want to show what we've been working on, too. Whether you've won or lost, ask the others what they were doing; some may not want to say (it can be very embarrassing to have five Jokers and not win—trust us, many of us have been there), but talking about our hopes for a hand is part of the Mah Jongg experience. Do congratulate the winner.

Be sure you place your Jokers in the middle of your exposure, if possible. It makes it easier for other players to know which exposure your Joker belongs to, and which tile to "pray to get!"

Make sure you separate your exposures on the rack, allowing others to clearly understand what they are. That's the price of calling for a discard. But there's no reason to lay out your exposures according to the order on the card—mix it up and keep the others on their toes. Only if you win should you put it in the correct order.

If you keep winning, be gracious about it. Nobody wants to play with a braggart. Mah Jongg is a game of skill, but there certainly is luck involved.

Table Rules

Table rules are very different from tournament rules, and a departure from official NMJL rules. We will touch upon just a few.

Whenever people get together, they develop their own way of doing things, and playing Mah Jongg is no exception. Table rules are the way that a particular group agrees to play, and there's a lot of variability. So the first thing you should do as a player who's new to a group is to ask, "Is there anything special about the way you play together?" Sometimes others will be quick to mention what they do, but other times you'll just see it when something comes up.

There can be rules about the Hot Wall. If you're playing for money, many play that a hand won in the Hot Wall gets double the regular payout. If there's a wall game, some players keep a dish where everyone puts in a quarter. The winner of the next game wins those quarters, too.

In some of our groups we "**Mish**" (rhymes with dish) after the final optional Charleston pass, and we usually let East make that decision. In the Mish, players put their unwanted tiles, five at most, face down in the middle of the table, where they're mixed; then players take out as many as they've put it. This differs between groups, but we always have the same laugh: it seems whatever tiles we put into the Mish, we get right back. Given that hope springs eternal, we keep trying!

G&T Time:

Toby: Table Rules, or House Rules, are made up. They don't exist in any book. All of us have quirky things we do when we play. In my group, we play that on the last wall, the Hot Wall, all winnings are doubled. Then all of our winnings go into OUR bank. I'm the banker and I send out quarterly reports with a tagline, «In order to increase our profitability, it is advisable to play more.» This way we get to go to a fabulous restaurant and drink Champagne. We have our priorities!

Gregg: I don't really care about playing for money, I just like playing the game, and of course I hope to win from time to time. (OK, truth: at least one out of four games—beating the odds!) One friend loves to play for money. When we're at her house, we have to bring quarters, and we never can do the Mish.

So congratulations! You are now "in the know" about etiquette and table rules. You are ready to meet the Mah Jongg world....

Afterword

You've started down the Mah Jongg path. You already know what a fun escape the game can be, but it has some less obvious benefits as well. It's an excellent way to give several parts of your brain a workout all at the same time, making you exercise those "little grey cells" that Agatha Christie's Hercule Poirot refers to so frequently. Every hand you're dealt forces you to analyze, categorize, and make assessments—and adjustments—until the game is over. No wonder you can't think about other things when you're playing!

A little lesson in neurology (oh, the unexpected places you'll go when you start to learn Mah Jongg!); we'll begin with some basics. Your brain has two hemispheres, the left and the right, both with very different functions. The left brain helps you with logic, details, and problem-solving. The right brain deals with the big picture, symbols, and possibilities. You can easily grasp how these get used while playing, but there's another area that enters the picture as well: the prefrontal cortex, which aids in social behavior and interactions. So even if you don't accomplish the goal of winning your hand, you've gained something.

There are a number of ways you might make the most of your time at the table, by playing different hands and varying the sets. If you don't really care about winning each time, try going for hands that are a bit more work. Stretch yourself. See if you can win each hand on the card, as seasoned players do. We also think it can only help players to familiarize themselves with several different kinds of sets, adding to one's mental conditioning. We know when we play with a set that's new to us, we have to use a bit more brain power to see what we've been dealt, and the possible directions to take. An idea: if you play with friends, why not see if everyone in the group can get a different set? It'll add to the fun.

We hope the paper set in this book has gotten you to this point, but it won't last forever. It was designed to help you get familiar with some of the lovely images you can find on various game tiles, and we hope that we've whet your appetite. It's time for you to find one of your own, but we urge you not to buy the first one you see. Find one you *like*.

There are always big online retailers who will happily sell you a set for very little money. Many even offer next-day delivery. We think everyone should have a set they're not worried about, one where, if a tile falls and breaks, it can easily be replaced. But for your own enjoyment, if you can, treat yourself to something special, something that makes your heart sing. (Some of these may cost only a bit more than the run-of-the-mill sets.) There are specialized online dealers who cater to MJ players, offering sets with unique colors and designs. Sometimes the backs of the tiles are special, or the tile faces. Find one that appeals to you. Feel a connection. Actually, when you think about it, you'll spend hundreds of hours with your mahjong set, enjoying time with others, socializing, and deepening friendships. These tiles will become part of your relationship with the game, and having a set that brings a smile to your lips is wonderful.

If you want something vintage, take your time with that as well. If you decide to buy one (we consider "vintage" any set that's older than we are!), there's so much to explore.

Yes, they're more expensive, but many of us feel these treasures are well worth the price. If you don't mind a bit of irregularity (we like to call this "part of the charm"), an older, loved set might well be the one for you. Look at eBay to see what's out there. Check out some of the wonderful websites where vintage sets are offered, or even just on display. Learn about different types of sets and materials. Are there certain types of tiles you like, be they bamboo, bone with bamboo, French ivory, Bakelite or Catalin, Lucite, or some other plastic? Do you want the faces to be white and easy to read? Do you prefer lovely shades of yellow or orange? Do you desire something hand-carved, with all the small variations that come with that? There's so much to decide, and you don't have to rush. Spend time familiarizing yourself with the different kinds of pieces that have brought happiness to others before you. If you want "old" but don't want imperfections, there are lots of "newer" sets that might fulfill that need, sets made after 1971, with the right number of Jokers and Flowers. These tend to be more uniform in appearance.

When starting out, don't make the mistake so many other beginners have made: buying a vintage set that's missing tiles. Many of us feel it will be easy to find pieces to make our sets whole. Not true!! It can take years to make a set playable, if it's even possible. Leave that job to people who specialize in restoring sets. Use your time to enjoy playing the game.

We adore lovely new sets as well as older ones. Whichever way you go, consider these pieces wonderful new friends, and treat them with respect: don't dump them onto the table, or allow others to flip them in the air with their card in order to "wash" them well; they'll get damaged. Create your own memories with your set, starting from the first game. These tiny pieces of art will soon find a place in your heart.

We wish you, your friends, and your family many hours of happiness around the Mah Jongg table. The pastime has enriched our lives so much—in ways we never expected—and we trust it will do the same for you.

Enjoy!

Gregg and Toby

About the Team

Gregg Swain grew up in New York City and developed a love of art. She majored in Art History at college and she earned a Doctorate in Clinical Psychology. She feels Mah Jongg combines these two interests. Intrigued by the art on vintage sets when she learned to play in 2010, she set out to research the images. Her book *Mah Jongg: The Art of the Game* is the first to showcase art created by craftsmen over the last hundred years. Gregg has taught scores of students to play The Game of Clattering Sparrows. She's lectured throughout North America about all aspects of the game. When Redstone Games wanted to develop their online mahjong solitaire game based on real tiles, they turned to her. Gregg's a frequent contributor to news stories about different aspects of the pastime. Her website, **www.MahjongTreasures.com**, has been viewed by hundreds of thousands of people around the world.

Toby Salk is a transplanted New Yorker and long time Berkeley resident who's taught Mah Jongg for over ten years to hundreds of students. Her grandmother, mother and aunts all played Mah Jongg before she was born so you might say she first heard the clicking and clacking of Mah Jongg tiles in the womb. A product of the 1960s and a great believer in community, Toby is the founder of a monthly brunch for Mah Jongg players. People come from all over to be a part of this boisterous and fun event. Toby currently teaches and lectures in private homes, ladies' clubs and Rancho La Puerta in Mexico. She also collects and restores vintage Mah Jongg sets. You can find her at **www.mahjonggforeveryone.com** or write to her at tobysmj@gmail.com.

Woody Swain is an art director and design consultant who worked at Madison Avenue ad agencies. He's lectured on graphic design, and won awards for his work for national print and TV. He can honestly say his artwork is on posters that have appeared all over the world, ranging from the sides of buses in Moscow to bus stops in Malawi. He's designed a number of books, including *Mah Jongg: The Art of the Game*. Woody resides in Manhattan with his wife Gregg. Find him at **www.WoodySwain.com**.

Gladys Grad is a well-known name in the American Mah Jongg community. Following her professional career in the Chicagoland area as a City Manager and university professor, she and her late husband Phil Klinsky acquired Mah Jongg Madness® (MJM) in 2005. MJM has grown to include annual tournament events with up to 450 participants each—primarily weekend getaways and cruises. Gladys codified Standardized National Mah Jongg Tournament Rules, and introduced Mah Jongg Master Points, a web-based system that formulates and ranks tournament players. In 2015, Gladys invented Siamese Mah Jongg® for 2-handed games. Now a 3- and 4-handed Royale Siamese Mah Jongg® version has followed, played throughout the world... complete with its own web-based game, and annual card with new hands. Siamese tournaments pop up everywhere Mah Jongg is played. Gladys also volunteers by helping local charities and organizations conduct their mahjong events. You can find her at **www.Mahjongg.org**.

Appendix A

Siamese Mah Jongg

"Each player uses two racks"

You'll love this simple yet very challenging and fun version of Mah Jongg! It allows just two people to play, with each player hoping to get Mah Jongg *twice.* Below is how to play the easiest version of "Siamese." For more information on different variations and tournament play, consult **www.Mahjongg.org** or our book's website.

Both players face each other, with two racks in front of each of them. They throw the dice to see who's East. They wash the tiles and then pick: East gets 28 and the opposite player 27. They leave the shuffled unpicked tiles on one side of the table, and put the discards on the other.

Each player arranges their tiles in both racks, as many on each rack as they like, and exchange tiles back and forth between racks. It doesn't matter how many tiles are on each rack at any one time. There is no Charleston.

East discards the 28th tile to begin the game. Then the opposite player picks their first tile from the table, discards a tile, and so on. Picking and discarding proceeds. Play is similar to four-person play. Players can call for discards, and make exposures. Once an exposure is made on a rack, all other exposures for that hand must be made on that same rack, but any tiles—even those not related to that exposure—may be kept on the angled lip of that rack. Players may exchange Jokers from their own or their opponents' exposures, up until the time the first Mah Jongg is declared; thereafter those Jokers are no longer available.

When Mah Jongg is achieved, that player discards and play recommences. Play ends when a player has won twice or when there are no more tiles left to pick.

Strategy's involved, but it's different from four-person Mah Jongg. You may have Mah Jongg but you might not want to call it. If you delay declaring MJ and exposing those tiles, you have longer to exchange your own Jokers or use them elsewhere. Once a Mah Jongg hand has been declared and exposed, the Jokers in the MJ exposures cannot be exchanged. The disadvantage of not exposing MJ is the game might finish before you have declared Mah Jongg, and you must have Mah Jongg exposed to win and be paid.

The rules for a dead hand are the same as in the four-person version. If a player has one dead hand exposed, that player may continue to exchange the remaining tiles between the two racks, but may not take from the Dead hand's exposures.

Payment is made at the end of the game(s) and is paid based on the number of MJs players have and the values on the NMJL Card. If you have two MJs, value on the second hand is doubled. If you declare two MJs at the same time, values are doubled.

G&T Time:

Gregg: Thank you, Gladys Grad, for inventing this style of play. Readers, play it with a friend to learn the card.
Toby: It's a fun way to exercise your brain.

Appendix B

Resources

The most important resource for playing the game we love is the National Mah Jongg League. They sell the Card, which you must have for play. The back of the Card gives you updated information about any rule and scoring changes. The League sells items you might want or need, including card protectors, sets, and "helping hands." The NMJL will answer questions by mail if you send a stamped, self-addressed envelope. Their website is **www.nationalmahjonggleague.org**.

Our website is the place to turn to find sellers of vintage sets, joker stickers, and up-to-date answers to questions in this book. There's also a lot more information about MJ history. Gladys Grad has provided us with detailed information about Siamese play and tournament rules at **www.Mahjongg.org**.

G&T Time:

Gregg: Toby and I both love old sets. We feel the history of the people who owned them and played with the tiles. We know how important those times around the table were.
Toby: I have my grandmother's set; it became my mother's, and it's bequeathed to my goddaughter. The set is a part of my family.

Appendix C

Glossary

A

Atomic A win with seven pairs of tiles, not part of NMJL play.

AUT Short for Autumn on a Flower. In NMJL play, a Flower is a Flower.

B

Bakelite A plastic sometimes used in vintage mahjong sets.

Bam One of the three suits. Short for Bamboo.

Bettor If there are five players, one can sit out and be the Bettor, guessing at the end of the Charleston who'll win. If right, the same amount paid to the winner will be paid to the Bettor.

Blind Pass A pass done only on the First Left or the Last Right of the Charleston. Any player can pass zero, one or two tiles and take (steal) a tile/s from the right or left pass to make a pass of three tiles. If a player looks at the tiles they're "stealing," they're considered dead and out of that game.

Bone sticks Long sticks with Dots on them made (typically) of cow bone and used in Asian-style play for betting.

Breaking the Wall East rolls the dice at the very beginning of the game. The number on the dice will determine where East's wall is broken. Tiles to the right are brought back to East's rack, and those to the left are dealt.

Breaking up a hand A player sacrifices their hand to prevent throwing a tile that will help another player. This usually happens toward the end of the game.

C

Call A player can "call" a tile at any time, providing it will complete the group they are playing on the card.

card Any card outlining hands to play, including ours

Card (the Card) The National Mah Jongg League publishes "the Card" every April 1, detailing that year's hands. **Our Card** exists in this book.

Casein A milk-based protein used to make plastic tiles.

Catalin Another plastic often used to make vintage tiles.

Charleston The passes at the beginning of the game, allowing all players to pass unwanted tiles and hopefully get some they need.

Circle One of the three suits, called Dot in American-style games.

Coffin A little container with a sliding lid that holds dice.

Courtesy Pass The optional last (7th) across pass, where one to three tiles may be passed.

Concealed A Concealed hand, abbreviated **C** on the card, indicates that you cannot "Call" for a tile except for Mah Jongg.

Crak One of the three suits, a short version of Character, the Chinese word on the tile.

D

Dead A player who has made an error and is

no longer in the game, or a tile that is no longer playable for that game.

Dead Hand When either a player has the wrong number of tiles, their exposure indicates they've made a mistake, or they can't win. Other players should call the hand dead.

Deal The distribution of the tiles at the start of the game. Typically each player takes their own.

Dealer Also known as East.

Defensive Play When players actively discard so as not to help anyone else win.

Discard An unwanted tile named and placed on the table by a player.

Doubles A House Rule in which winners get twice the value of the hand when doubles have been thrown on the dice for that game.

Dot One of the three suits, also called a Circle.

Down A discarded tile, either on the table or with its whole name said, which cannot be reclaimed by the discarder.

E

East 1. One of the Winds. 2. The person who "starts" the game.

Exposure When a tile is called, the player must place it, along with the other tiles completing the grouping, on top of their rack. This is the exposure.

Exposed 1. A tile that has been "called" and placed on the rack. 2. A visible hand, indicated by an **X** on the cards, that allows players to call for its tiles.

F

First Left The mandatory three-tile third pass in the Charleston.

Final Right The last mandatory pass of the second cycle of the Charleston.

Flowers Specific tiles—that don't necessarily have flowers on them. They can have any number, partial word or image other than a dragon or a bird. A Flower is a Flower, and NMJL play calls for eight.

G

Green Green Dragon. May have an **F** ("Fa") for "prosperity." Goes with the Bams.

Grouping Required number of particular tiles for a hand.

H

Hand A combination of tiles from the Card. Each line on the Card is a different hand.

Honors A name for the Winds and Dragons.

Hop Toi Hop Toi is called when tiles are picked from two walls during the dealing of the tiles, e.g., the 19th stack from one wall and the first stack from the second wall.

Hot Wall The last short wall in front of East, signaling the game is about to end.

Hot Tile A tile that has not been discarded yet, thought risky to discard.

House Rules The rules that many groups make up for themselves.

J

Joker A wild tile that can stand in for any tile—if it's part of a group of three or more identical tiles.

Joker Exchange When a Joker is part of an exposure, and another player has the natural tile it represents, the player can ask for the Joker in exchange for the natural tile, on their turn, after they have picked and racked. A discard follows. There is no need to show how the Joker will be used.

K

Kitty The money you bring with you to the game for betting. It can be your money purse.

Kong A group of four identical tiles. You can use up to four Jokers.

L

Last Right Also known as Final Right in the Charleston.

League Nickname for the National Mah Jongg League.

M

Mah-Jongg The game's name as trademarked by Joseph P. Babcock. Other names for original versions include: Mahjong, Mahjongg, Ma Jong, Ma Chong, Ma Chiang, Ma Deuck, Pung Chow, Pe-Ling, the Game of a Thousand Intelligences, Mah Cheuk, Chung Fa, and the Game of Clattering Sparrows.

Maven A Yiddish word to describe an expert.

Mia When playing with three players, the name often given to the empty seat (for MIA).

Mish A house rule. At the end of the Charleston, players can put up to five unwanted tiles into the center of the table and mix them. Each removes the number of tiles they put in. Also known as **Mush**.

N

NMJL Acronym for the National Mah Jongg League.

National Mah Jongg League The governing body of this style of play. They publish the Card each April outlining the new hands.

N

Neutral Can be used with any kind of tile.

O

Opposite Player The player across the table from a player.

Optional Pass *See* Courtesy Pass.

P

Pair Two identical tiles. You can never use a Joker in a pair.

Pass 1. A synchronized tile exchange, as done during the Charleston. 2. The tiles given and taken during the Charleston, when typically three unwanted tiles are switched for others. (*Also see* Blind Pass)

Pick To take the next tile from the wall.

Pip The "dots" on a die.

Pung Three identical tiles in a group. Up to three Jokers may be used.

Pushke The purse or bag where you keep your winnings.

Pretty An old name for Flower.

Pusher A long device typically attached to a rack to help push a wall out toward the middle of the table.

Q

Quarter On the NMJL Card, there is a value at the end of every line. This amount indicates the money the winner will get from each player (often a quarter).

Quint Five identical tiles in a group. Except with Flowers, you must use a Joker to complete this group.

R

Rack 1. The piece that holds a player's tiles. 2. To place your tile on your rack.

Racking Placing a picked tile on the angled lip of the rack.

Red Red Dragon. May have a **C** ("Chung") for "center." Goes with the Craks.

Rod Another term for Bamboo.

ROLLOR The acronym used to help with the order of the passes in the Charleston. Right Opposite Left, Left Opposite Right.

Royale Siamese Mah Jongg A four-handed version of Siamese Mah Jongg.

S

Seasons Often seen on Flower tiles: SUM, AUT, WIN, SPR. A Flower is a Flower.

Second Left The Second Left—with tiles

stacked two layers high—signals the optional second set of Charleston passes. Any player can stop the exchanges right before this point, as long as no one has looked at their second pass.

Section A category on the card. Words and numbers in bold denote each section.

Self-Pick A player picks their own tile to call "Mah Jongg!"

Sextet Six identical tiles in a group. Except with Flowers, you must use at least two Jokers to complete this group.

Shark An expert player.

Siamese Mah Jongg A way to play the game with only two people, invented by Gladys Grad.

Single One tile, or a tile in a group that does not match the other tiles. Example: NEWS has single tiles, as do all the Years: 2020, etc. No Jokers allowed.

Soap Another name for a White Dragon.

SPR Short for Spring on a Flower. A Flower is a Flower.

Stack A group of two tiles, two tiles high.

Stealing Taking one or more tiles from those just passed in the Charleston, without looking, and passing that along as part of a Blind Pass. This may only happen on the First Left and Final Right. Any player can pass zero, one or two tiles and take a tile/s from the right or left pass to make a pass of three tiles.

Sticks Another name for Bams.

Stopper The piece on the rack's outside left edge, used for building the wall.

Stopping the Charleston Any player can decide not to continue the passes, but only after the First Left. If any player has looked at the Second Left, it's too late.

SUM Short for Summer on a Flower. A Flower is a Flower.

T

Table Rules Rules made up by a group of players.

Take Another word for Call, used to claim a discard.

Tile A game piece for Mah Jongg, made from virtually any material: paper, cardboard, metal, plastic, bone, bamboo, Lucite, ivory, mother of pearl….

V

Value The number at the end of each line of a card indicating how much the hand's worth.

Vintage Set A set typically made before 1970.

W

Wall The row of tiles in front of each person's rack or that have been pushed out into the center of the table.

Washing the Tiles When all players use their hands to carefully mix the tiles, facedown on the table, before the walls are built.

Wall Game No one wins the game.

White A White Dragon. May have the letter **B** (for "Bai") or **P** (for "Po") on it meaning "pure." Goes with the Dots, but it's also neutral when used as a zero in the year hands.

WIN Short for Winter on a Flower. A Flower is a Flower.

Winds North East West and South tiles. Part of the Honors group, and neutral.

Y

Year Hand A hand reflecting the card's year, such as 2021, 2022, 2023, etc.

Z

Zero A Soap (or White Dragon) is a zero only in the context of a year, i.e., 2020, and in this use it's neutral.

Appendix D

Mah Jongg Card

Tape this edge to the other green-starred edge.

★
★

To accompany

American Mah Jongg for Everyone: The Complete Beginner's Guide

by Gregg Swain and Toby Salk

Adapted with permission from the NMJL.

Cut the card pieces out and tape them at the "X" marks to create a tri-fold card.

Note: White Dragon serves as a zero "0." It may be used with any suit.

21st CENTURY	**VALUES**
222 1111 222 1111 (Any 2 Suits)	x 25
NNNN E W SSSS 22 11 (These Nos. Only; Same Suit)	x 25
FF 2222 1111 0000 (Any 2 Suits)	x 25
NEWS 222 111 0000 or NEWS 222 111 0000 (Any 1 or 2 Suits)	c 30

2 4 6 8	
22 44 DDDD 666 888 (Any 2 Suits and Non-matching Dragons)	x 25
22 44 66 8888 8888 (3 Suits)	x 25
22 44 444 666 8888 (3 Suits)	x 25
222 444 6666 8888 (Any 1 Suit)	x 25
222 888 DDDD DDDD (3 Suits)	x 25
FF 222 444 666 888 (Any 1 Suit)	c 30

LIKE NUMBERS	
FF 1111 1111 1111 (Any Like Nos.)	x 25
11 DD 111 DDD 1111 (3 Suits; Any Like Nos.)	c 30

ADDITION: HEAVENLY 11s	
FFFF 5555+6666=11 or FFFF 5555 + 6666=11 (1 or 3 Suits)	x 25
FFFF 4444+7777=11 or FFFF 4444 + 7777=11 (1 or 3 Suits)	x 25
FFFF 3333+8888=11 or FFFF 3333 + 8888=11 (1 or 3 Suits)	x 25

★ ★ ★ Tape this edge to the other blue-starred edge.

QUINTS	VALUES
22 333 4444 55555 (Any 1 Suit; These Nos. Only)	x 45
11111 2222 33333 or 11111 2222 33333 (1 or 3 Suits; Any Consec. Nos.)	x 45
FFFF NNNNN 11111 (Any Wind, Any No.)	x 45
FFFF DDDDD 11111 (Any Dragon, Any No.)	x 45

CONSECUTIVE RUN

11 222 3333 444 55 or 55 666 7777 888 99 (Any 1 Suit)	x 25
111 2222 333 4444 (Any 2 Suits; 4 Consec. Nos.)	x 25
★ FFFF 1111 2222 DD or FFFF 1111 2222 DD (1 or 3 Suits; Any Consec. Nos.)	x 25
★ 11 22 111 222 3333 (3 Suits; Any Consec. Nos.)	x 25
★ 1111 22 22 22 3333 (Any 3 Consec. Nos.; Pairs Middle No. Only)	x 25
111 22 333 DDD DDD (Any 3 Consec. Nos.; Non-matching Dragons)	c 30

1 3 5 7 9

11 333 5555 777 99 (Any 1 Suit)	x 25
111 3333 333 5555 or 555 7777 777 9999 (Any 2 Suits)	x 25
FFFF 1111 33 5555 or FFFF 1111 33 5555 (1 or 3 Suits)	x 25
FFFF 5555 77 9999 or FFFF 5555 77 9999 (1 or 3 Suits)	x 25
FF 1111 9999 DDDD or FF 1111 9999 DDDD (1 or 3 Suits)	x 25
11 333 DDDD 333 55 or 55 777 DDDD 777 99 (3 Suits)	x 25
111 3 555 555 7 999 (Any 2 Suits)	c 30

Tape this edge to the other blue-starred edge.

WINDS AND DRAGONS	VALUES
NNNN EEEE WWWW SS	x 25
FF DDDD NEWS DDDD (Any 2 Dragons)	x 25
NNNN SSSS 111 111 (Any 2 Suits; Pungs Any like Odd No. Only)	c 25
EEEE WWWW 222 222 (Any 2 Suits; Pungs Any like Even No. Only)	c 25
FF DDDD DDDD DDDD	x 25

3 6 9

3333 66 9999 DDDD (Any 1 Suit)	x 25
FF 3333 6666 9999 or FF 3333 6666 9999 (1 or 3 Suits)	x 25
33 66 99 3333 3333 (3 Suits; Kongs 3s, 6s, or 9s)	x 25
333 666 9999 9999 (3 Suits; Kongs, 9s Only)	c 25

SINGLES AND PAIRS

NN EE WW SS 11 11 22 (3 Suits, These Nos. Only)	c 50
FF 11 22 33 44 55 DD (Any 1 Suit; Any 5 Consec. Nos.)	c 50
FF 22 44 66 88 22 88 (Any 2 Suits; Last Pairs only 2s and 8s)	c 50
11 33 55 77 99 11 11 (Last 2 Pairs; Any like Odd No.)	c 50
FF 11 22 11 22 11 22 (Any 2 Consec. Nos.)	c 50
336 33669 336699 (All 3 Suits)	c 50
FF 2019 2020 2021 (Any 3 Consec. Years in 21st Century; 3 Suits)	c 75

The Card is provided for instructional use only. To play Mah Jongg, you need to purchase an official card from the National Mah Jongg League. For more information, visit the National Mah Jongg League website at **www.nationalmahjonggleague.org**

Tape this edge to the other green-starred edge.

★★

Appendix E

Cut out these tiles for play.

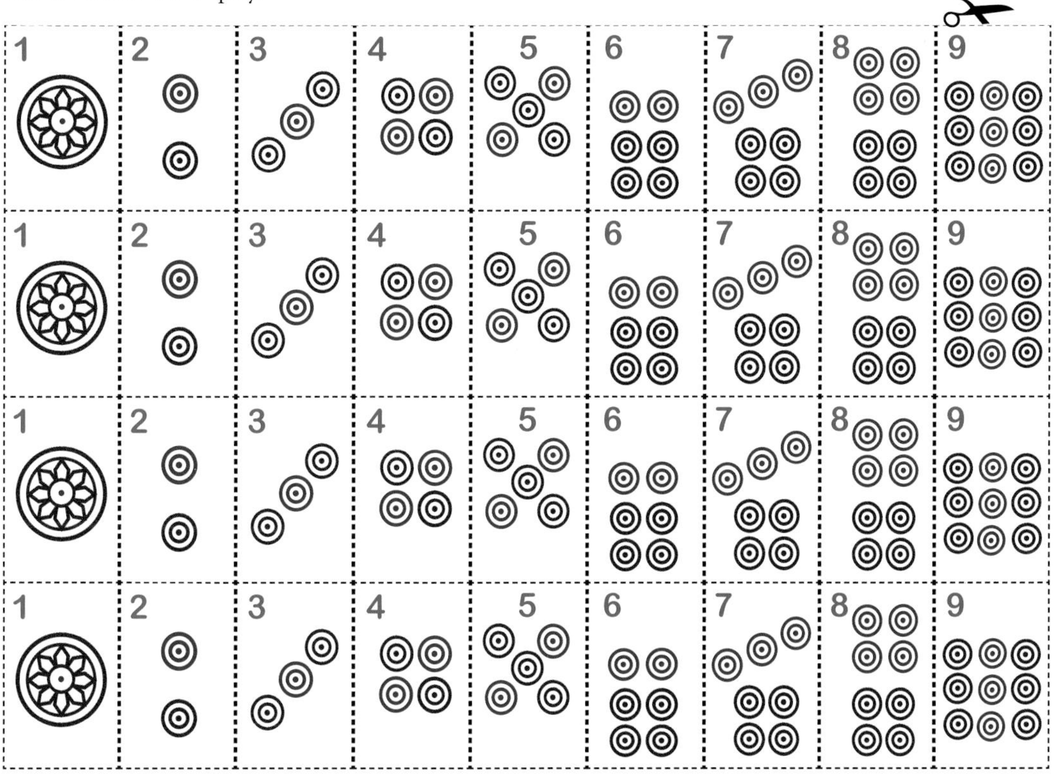

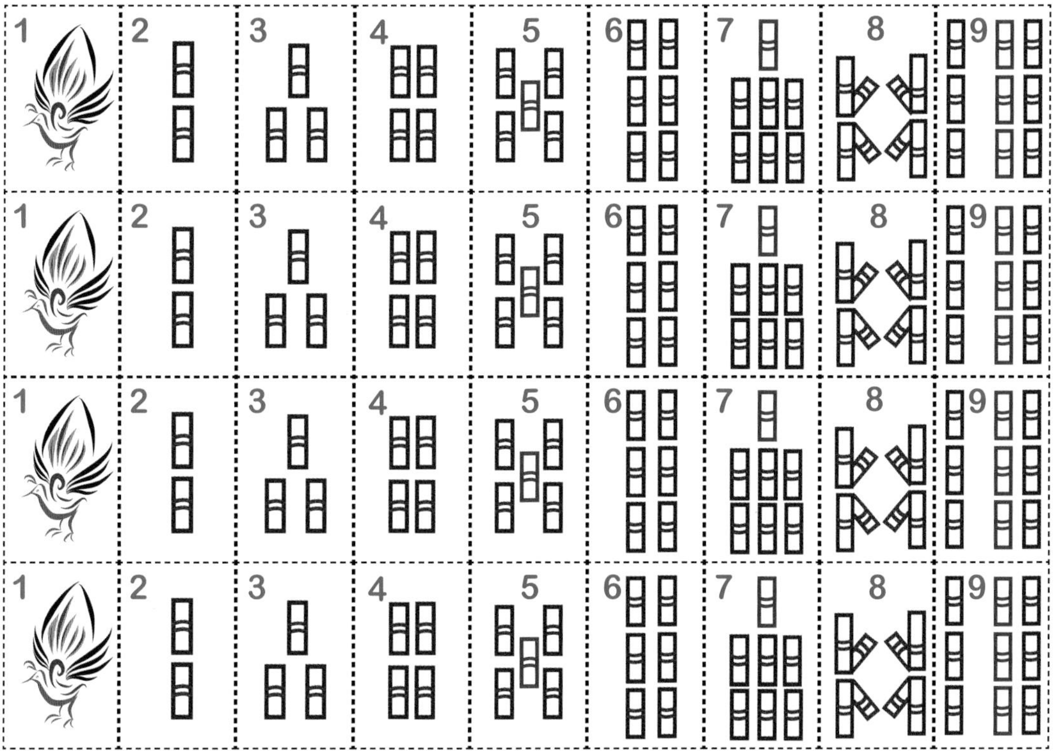

Cut out these tiles for play.